# DON'T GET BITTEN

### The Dangers of Things
### That Bite or Sting

# DON'T GET BITTEN

## The Dangers of Things That Bite or Sting

*Buck Tilton, M.S.*

THE MOUNTAINEERS BOOKS

Published by
The Mountaineers Books
1001 SW Klickitat Way, Suite 201
Seattle, WA 98134

First edition, 2003
No part of this book may be reproduced in any form, or by any electronic, mechanical, or other means, without permission in writing from the publisher.

Published simultaneously in Great Britain by Cordee, 3a DeMontfort Street, Leicester, England, LE1 7HD

Manufactured in Canada

Project Editor: Laura Drury
Copyeditor: Kris Fulsaas
Cover and Book Design: The Mountaineers Books
Layout: Jennifer LaRock Shontz
Illustrator: Moore Creative Design
Cover illustration: Mayumi Thompson

*Library of Congress Cataloging-in-Publication Data*
Tilton, Buck.
   Don't get bitten : the dangers of things that bite or sting / Buck Tilton.— 1st ed.
       p. cm.
Includes bibliographical references.
   ISBN 0-89886-907-2 (pbk.)
   1. Bites and stings—Prevention. 2. Dangerous animals. I. Title.
   RD96.2.T54 2003
   617.1—dc21
                                      2003001328

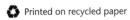 Printed on recycled paper

# *Contents*

# Introduction

*The goal of this little book is to provide the knowledge that will make your wilderness trips as totally safe from potentially dangerous bites and stings as possible.*

Why does the wild outdoors attract us so very much? Sorting through my thoughts and feelings, again and again, year after year, I am still unable to explain this clearly, even to myself. I am able to tell what attracts me—the breathtaking majesty of sky-seeking mountains, the quiet dignity of dusty deserts, the irresistible surge of mighty rivers, and on and on. I can say that I thrive on the absence of phone, computer, and television; and I can tell you how often wild land meets my need to be reminded of the basics of existence—water, food, shelter—and the basics of life: learning and enjoying. I find there, in wildness, proverbial peace and contentment, and a rich meaning for myself as a human inseparable from the whole of all things. Perhaps, in the end, I am simply and deeply in love with wilderness—and love is not only consuming but also, ultimately, inexplicable.

Honesty urges me to admit, however, that I am not in love with all the creatures of the wild outdoors. I do not even like some of them. Despite the undeniable thrill of the warning rattle of a western diamondback, I almost always prefer to travel well apart from snakes. I cannot fully engage myself, physically or spiritually, in the tickling crawl over my skin of anything with more legs than me, and I truly dislike pushing my face through a spider's web strung across a trail, innocent of my disgust as it may be. I am not really keen on scorpions, bees, wasps, yellow jackets, hornets, or fire ants either. And mosquitoes! Why, oh, why are there mosquitoes? Why can I not rise above their whine and stop allowing them to spoil otherwise utterly splendid terrain?

My sentiments echo those of multitudes of humans, from Alabama to Zimbabwe. There is no shortage of creatures not to like out there. Around 3000 species of snakes squirm across sand, through grass, into trees, and among rocks just about everywhere on Earth where they find temperatures they can tolerate. Of the phylum Arthropoda, which includes all invertebrate animals (including all bugs), there are nearly one million species, about 80 percent of all known animals. Within the class Arachnida, the eight-legged creatures of the world, a class of more than 60,000 total species, approximately 34,000 species are spiders and as many as 1400 species (experts disagree on the number) are scorpions. In prime habitat areas, authorities estimate the number of scurrying arachnids may run as high as a whopping 265,000 per acre. There are more than 3000 species of mosquitoes. There are about 3500 species in the order Hymenoptera, which includes bees and their relatives. A typical fire ant hill houses more than 25,000 individuals.

You understand. It is completely impossible to comprehend the total number of life forms that could be considered capably bothersome.

**Note:** This book concerns itself with animals no bigger than an eastern diamondback rattlesnake and as small as a viral particle. Larger creatures are left to other books. Smaller "creatures" do not exist within today's scope of knowledge.

## MORE THAN BOTHERSOME

Dislike of the creatures discussed in this book originates not so much because they can be an annoyance but more, sometimes much more, from the fact they might bite (with their front parts) or sting (with their back parts), and it sometimes hurts more than a little bit. Some arthropods cause little or no pain but leave wounds that itch horribly. Humans are the favored source of food for some arthropods, and some of those set up housekeeping on and/or within human skin. Dislike may reach fear-and-loathing proportions when you remember that the pain, big or small, could be followed by serious damage or death from venom or germs these animals may leave inside you. But what, truly, are the risks to humans, especially to wilderness travelers? And how can those risks be reduced to a minimum? That is what this book is all about.

### Fascinating Facts

It would nice, from a statistical point of view, to be able to state precisely that X number of humans were bitten by Y species and Z of those people died. Those numbers do not exist because medical care providers are not required to report patients who were treated for many bites and stings—thus there are no records.

CHAPTER 1.

# *Dangerous Reptiles*

**IMAGINE THIS:**
*In the dark, reaching into a pile of dead tree limbs for fuel for your small fire, you feel a sharp sting near the base of your thumb. Within minutes the burning pain at the bite site has started a searing crawl up your arm. Over the next hour blood oozes from two fang marks. Your hand starts to bulge as swelling extends outward from the bite. And you are alone. What are you going to do?*

Generally speaking, snakes put considerable effort into avoiding humans and bite only when they feel threatened. But if they do bite, an estimated 15 percent of the 3000 species of snakes on planet Earth may be considered potentially dangerous to human beings. Some of the best guesses by experts place the number of deaths each year, worldwide, as high as 50,000. Data offers unreliable statistics because snakebites are not reportable injuries, but this much is sure: Few of these deaths occur in the United States.

### A Closer Look: When Do Snakes Bite?
At dawn and dusk, during the warmest months—April to September in the United States—when snakes are most active (and humans, perhaps, more careless), you are most likely to get bitten.

Out of an estimated 7000 to 8000 or so venomous snake-bites per year in the United States, there may be, when the snakes have a good year, say some experts, fifteen bites fatal to humans. The number probably stands much lower for most recent years—five to six deaths per year, say some experts. Between 1983 and 1998, however, only ten deaths caused by bites of venomous snakes were reported to the Poison Control Centers of the United States. The low number of deaths can be accredited, most likely, to the availability of effective antivenins and the relatively low toxicity of the venom of U.S. snakes.

### A Closer Look: Who Do Snakes Bite?

Snakebites occur most often to the lower extremities, with upper extremities coming in second. Upper-extremity bites are usually from a harassed snake—someone tries to kill it, capture it, or otherwise handle it. The most common profile of a bitten human in the United States is a young, intoxicated male, seventeen to twenty-seven years old, who intentionally messes with a pit viper.

At least 99 out of every 100 poisonous bites by indigenous snakes in the United States are those of a pit viper, family Viperidae: rattlesnakes, copperheads, and water moccasins (or cottonmouths). The other 1 out of 100 bites usually comes from a coral snake, family Elapidae, but a few bites are received from exotic snakes kept as pets. Almost all the fatalities caused by snakes in the United States occur after a bite from either an eastern or western diamondback. Those who are bitten and that die are either very young, very old, or unable to find a source of antivenin.

### Important Note

Many of the symptoms of a snakebite are directly proportional to the fear the victim experiences. If bitten, it is decidedly in your best interest to stay as calm as possible.

**Table 1.1**

### Venomous Snakes of the World

| Family | Subfamily | Examples | Characteristics |
|--------|-----------|----------|-----------------|
| Viperidae | Crotalinae | All the pit vipers:<br>Bushmasters<br>Copperheads<br>Cottonmouths<br>Fer-de-lances<br>Rattlesnakes<br>etc. | Heat-sensitive pit between eye and nostril; catlike pupils; retractable fangs |
| Viperidae | Viperinae | All the true vipers:<br>Gaboon vipers<br>Puff adders<br>Russell's vipers<br>Saw-scaled vipers<br>etc. | No heat-sensitive pit |
| Elapidae |  | Cobras<br>Coral snakes<br>Kraits<br>Mambas<br>etc. | Short, fixed fangs; chewing sometimes required to inject venom |
| Hydrophidae |  | All true sea snakes:<br>Pelagic sea snake<br>etc. | Fangs similar to snakes in Elapidae family |

Facts about the number of lizard bites in the United States are even less reliable than data for snakebites. In all the world, however, only two species of lizards are venomous. Both are found in North America, and both are of the genus *Heloderma*. One, the Gila monster, is common in the United States.

## PIT VIPERS

Of at least thirty-four species of pit vipers in North America, by far the most common are rattlesnakes, and they are widely dispersed throughout the country. All rattlesnakes are pit vipers (subfamily Crotalinae)—but not all pit vipers have rattles. Copperheads and water moccasins (cottonmouths) are rattleless, and newborn rattlesnakes cannot make the distinctive "buzz" until after their first molting (shedding of skin), even though they can bite and inject venom prior to growing grown-up rattles. All pit vipers do have distinctly triangular heads, catlike pupils, heat-sensitive pits between eyes and nostrils (thus the name "pit viper"), and two very special fangs.

### Important Note

Pit vipers come in all sorts of sizes, colors, and distinctive patterns along their lengths. It is beyond the scope of this little book to attempt to describe them specifically. Check with local experts to learn descriptions of local dangerous snakes in areas where you intend to travel.

A pit viper's fangs are hinged to swing downward at a 90-degree angle from the upper jaw. At rest, the fangs fold against the roof of the snake's mouth. At unrest, the jaw opens alarmingly wide and the fangs drop into striking position, allowing the venom to be ejected by muscular contraction down canals within the fangs and into the tissue of a prey or enemy when the snake bites (see Figure 1.1). Both the upright position of the fangs and the injection of venom are controlled by the "will" of the snake: It can open its mouth without showing the fangs, and it can bite without injecting venom. In short, pit vipers have the most sophisticated venom delivery system in the snake world.

### Figure 1.1 Venom Delivery Apparatus of a Pit Viper

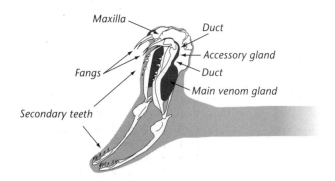

Somewhere between 75 and 80 percent of pit viper bites are associated with envenomization. Or, to say it another way, one out of every four to five bites is "dry": no venom injected. Why? We cannot say for sure. The snake may instinctively know that a human, even dead, will remain inedible and choose to save its venom for mealtime. How upset, startled, or frightened the snake is could also be a factor in whether it injects venom and, if it does, how much venom it injects. Pit viper venom, a very complex poison, acts aggressively on local tissue, "digesting" it, sort of, which makes the normal prey of the snake easier to process as food.

### Important Note

A dead, even decapitated pit viper can reflexively bite and inject venom for up to 1 hour after death.

### Facts about North American Pit Vipers

All species of pit vipers hit maximum crawl speed at about 3 miles per hour (5 kilometers/hour), no faster than an adult's determined walking rate. Pit vipers do not chase humans, although they may get confused and "run away" toward a human.

Pit vipers use their forked tongue only—and harmlessly—to detect chemical odors in the environment.

Pit viper fangs grow to no longer than 0.8 inch (20 millimeters) even in the largest rattlesnakes.

Pit vipers strike at a maximum speed of about 8 feet per second.

Pit vipers can strike distances of no more than approximately one-half their own body length.

Pit vipers, namely the eastern diamondback rattlesnake, can exceed 6.56 feet (2 meters) in length.

Pit vipers that have rattles do not always use them before they strike.

Pit viper babies are, perhaps, more likely to strike, but an adult snake can inject an average of seventeen times more venom than can a baby snake, and that makes the adult far more dangerous.

## A Closer Look: Pit Viper Danger Zones

As you move south geographically into warmer territory, you find increasing numbers of snakes and correspondingly increasing numbers of snake-bitten humans. The southwestern United States is the area where you are most likely to receive a snakebite. Historically, the five states in which you are most likely to receive a fatal snakebite, from most likely to least likely, are:

1. Arizona
2. Florida
3. Georgia
4. Texas
5. Alabama

### Signs and Symptoms

Whether a pit viper injects venom or no, all snakebite victims have in common one thing: a fang mark or marks. One fang mark means either the snake lost a fang prior to biting or missed with the other fang when it did bite. Two fang marks are more common. You may see small marks from the snake's secondary teeth as well. Systemic effects—things that happen away from the bite site—are also common.

How dangerous is pit viper venom to a human? The amount of venom and the toxicity of the venom are primary factors determining the risk to the victim. Poison from the Mojave rattlesnake, for instance, rates as approximately forty-four times more potent than the Southern copperhead's. Risk factors also include (1) the size and health of the snake; (2) the age, size, health, and emotional stability of the victim;

(3) where, anatomically, the victim was bitten; (4) how deep the fangs went; (5) what first aid is provided; and (6) what hospital care is provided.

The results of envenomization vary greatly depending on these variables. No precise way to differentiate the seriousness of a pit viper bite exists, but generally speaking the following can be said.

**Mild** pit viper envenomizations (about 35 percent of all envenomizations) usually cause severe burning pain within minutes. You can, however, not hurt much and still be significantly poisoned, depending mostly on the species that bit you. Within 30 to 60 minutes, other signs and symptoms may develop. Variable swelling progresses outward from the bite. Variable ecchymosis (black and blue bruising) often appears. Blood may keep oozing from the wound, a result of the anticoagulant effect of the venom. Common are nausea with or without vomiting, weakness, dizziness or faintness, sweating and chills, and numbness or tingling of the mouth, tongue, scalp, or feet. There may be a strange taste, such as "metallic" or "rubbery," in the mouth.

**Moderate** pit viper envenomizations (about 25 percent of the total) may include all the above symptoms, but worse, with the addition of swelling that moves up the arm or leg toward the heart and swollen lymph nodes along the way. Ecchymosis sometimes develops at anatomic locations somewhat remote from the bite.

**Severe** pit viper envenomizations (about 10 to 15 percent of the total) could be indicated by all the above symptoms, but even worse, and might also include big jumps in pulse and breathing rates, profound swelling, blurred vision, headache, and shock.

Another way to evaluate the severity of a pit viper bite is

this: The sooner the bad things start happening after the bite and the more profound the bad things, the worse the envenomization. Death is possible in severe cases.

**A Closer Look: What to Do If You Are Alone**

Alone and bitten by a pit viper? Follow all the victim management guidelines, with one exception: You should walk out slowly with frequent rest breaks. Do not wait around to see if you are going to swell up and/or die.

### Treatment

Antivenins are available, often readily, in hospitals near snake country. Until snakebite victims can reach a hospital, most will benefit from the treatment guidelines below, which have been developed especially for North American pit viper envenomization. Please note that there are almost as many *do not's* as there are *do's*. It is important to observe the *do not's* because otherwise they can make the victim quite a bit worse.

1. Calm and reassure the victim.
2. Keep the victim physically at rest with the bitten extremity immobilized and kept at approximately the same level as the heart. (Note: Some experts believe the snake-bitten extremity should be kept slightly lower than the victim's heart.)
3. Remove rings, watches, or anything else that might reduce the circulation if swelling occurs.
4. Wash the wound.
5. Measure the circumference of the extremity at the site of the bite and at a couple of sites between the bite and the heart, and monitor swelling.
6. Evacuate the victim by carrying, by going for help to

carry, or, if the victim is stable, by slow walking with frequent rest breaks.

7. If the victim is not moving (which produces heat), keep the victim warm.

8. Keep the victim well hydrated with clear fluids unless he or she develops pronounced vomiting.

9. Do not cut and suck. Mechanical suction (not oral suction) may be valuable. The sooner mechanical suction starts, the better. Suction should be applied, for best results, for 30 minutes using a negative-pressure venom extraction device and without cutting. To keep up the suction, monitor the device and reapply it when the suction fails, which it will keep doing. Such devices are available in many stores that sell outdoor products.

10. Do not give painkillers unless the victim is very stable, showing no signs of getting worse.

11. Do not apply ice or immerse the wound in cold water.

12. Do not apply a tourniquet.

13. Do not give the victim alcohol to drink.

14. Do not electrically shock the victim.

### A Closer Look: Pit Viper Antivenin

Old antivenins are made from horse serum, to which allergic reactions, sometimes severe, are common. The newest antivenin utilizes sheep serum and promises far fewer adverse reactions. In addition, the newest antivenin is more broadly targeted and should work for cottonmouth and copperhead bites instead of primarily for rattlesnake bites. The recommended dose for treating a victim with the newest antivenin is 12 to 18 vials. As of the year 2002, the recommended dose will set you back financially somewhere between $12,000 and $17,000.

## CORAL SNAKES

You can find coral snakes in Arizona, Texas, and the southeastern states in three subspecies that resemble each other very much. Brightly banded in red, yellow, and black, all coral snakes (subfamily Viperinae) of the United States are described by a particular color sequence: "Red on black, venom lack; red on yellow, kill a fellow." In other words, red bands bordered by yellow bands means the snake is dangerous.

### Important Note

From a very safe distance, try to identify any snake that bites, but do not attempt to catch the snake. Second victims are created by such behavior.

These snakes are shy, nonaggressive, and poorly adapted to bite humans. Coral snakes cannot strike out, as pit vipers do, so most bites are the reward a human receives for handling a coral snake. The short, fixed fangs in the front of a small mouth make it all but impossible for coral snakes to bite anything on humans other than a finger, a toe, or a fold in skin, and they almost always have to hang on and chew to do damage. You may have ample time, and you are well advised, to snatch off a chewing coral snake before it chews long enough to inject venom. Approximately 40 percent of coral snake bites envenom the bitten victim.

On the complexity scale, coral snake venom ranks much lower than pit viper venom. On the potency scale, however, the venom of these colorful reptiles is much higher. In the United States only the Mojave rattler has more potent venom than a coral snake, and one adult coral snake packs enough venom to kill four to five adult humans. It is fortunate that these snakes are poorly adapted to bite humans.

Experts disagree over the number of coral snake bites to humans occurring annually, with ranges varying from about twenty to about sixty. Who knows when the last human death from a bite occurred? It could have been as long ago as a confirmed death in 1959.

## Signs and Symptoms

Once bitten, the victim may or may not complain of pain, which is usually mild and soon goes away. Localized swelling is possible but not common. It takes as much as 12 to 13 hours for signs and symptoms to reach the point where the victim wants help. Then you might hear complaints of nausea followed by vomiting, often the earliest sign and symptom. Headache, stomach pain, and sweaty and pale skin are common. Be alert for dizziness, weakness, numbness, and difficulty speaking and/or swallowing. Respiratory difficulty and an altered mental status (such as drowsiness) are really bad signs. Despite the fact that deaths are rare, it is estimated that untreated coral snake bites may kill about 10 percent of those bitten.

## Treatment

Since significant signs and symptoms can be so long delayed, early evacuation of persons suspected of having been bitten by coral snakes is strongly advised. How you get them to a doctor does not seem to matter much, but speed does. Antivenin should be started as soon as possible to be most effective. Little first aid works other than keeping the patient calm and cleaning the wound—with one possible exception: the pressure-immobilization technique.

Developed in Australia, where there are numerous relatives of the coral snake—called elapids—pressure-immobilization involves securing elastic wraps (such as those used to secure sprained ankles) around the bite site, up the extremity, and back down the extremity, then followed with some type of splint (see Figure 1.2). Properly applied—with about the same

### Figure 1.2 The Pressure–Immobilization Technique

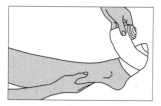

**a)** Starting from the toes, put a broad, firm bandage around the bitten area—don't take off any clothes such as jeans, but cut the seams if they can't be pushed out of the way, and keep the leg as still as possible while you are bandaging;

**b)** make the bandage as tight as for a sprained ankle;

**c)** bandage as much of the leg as possible, especially the toes;

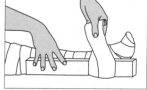

**d)** put a splint beside the bandage and bind that to the leg to help keep the leg still.

pressure as used for wrapping a sprained ankle—pressure-immobilization prevents the spread of elapid venom until a hospital can be found. It has proven very effective as a first-aid method for elapid bites in Australia, but remains untested on coral snake bites. It could, however, help a lot.

## GILA MONSTERS

Of the estimated 3000 species of lizards known today, it is somewhat surprising that only the Gila monster and the Mexican beaded lizard are venomous, despite plenty of mythology to the contrary. If undisturbed, Gila (pronounced HEE-lah) monsters live quiet and peaceful lives, hunting at night throughout much of the southwestern United States.

Gila monsters grow to a maximum length of about 1.67 feet (50 centimeters). They are essentially black with smears of yellow and/or pink. Built like weight lifters of the lizard world, they have especially massive jaw muscles. Their powerful jaws compensate for their primitive teeth and no means for injecting their poison. The venom glands of these lizards are in their lower jaws and not connected to their teeth (as they are in snakes). A Gila monster locks on when it bites, while the venom drools into the wound it creates, making removal of the lizard from your hand or foot highly advisable, though this is often difficult. They would not cause much pain when they bite except that they hang on so tightly and chew so hard.

Gila monsters never bite humans unless they are messed with—such as being picked up or stepped on—at which time they are capable of pivoting rapidly on their hind legs and lashing out with relatively incredible speed. It has been at least fifty years since a confirmed human death in the United States from a Gila monster bite—and some experts believe even that death might not have been from a Gila monster.

### Fascinating Facts

✔ Gila monsters do not have poisonous breath.
✔ They cannot spit their venom.
✔ They are not able to sting with their tails.
✔ When they bite, they hold on tightly, but it is a myth that they will let go when it thunders.

## Signs and Symptoms

Gila monster venom is comparable to some rattlesnake venom, but bleeding from the nasty wound of the bite may be initially more arresting. Pain, throbbing or burning, may radiate up the arm or leg. Envenomization may produce nausea and vomiting, dizziness, weakness, profuse sweating, and difficulty breathing.

## Treatment

To remove the Gila monster from the victim, you may likely be required to heat the underside of its jaws with matches or a lighter, place the attached lizard under a flow of hot water, or pry open its jaws with some instrument to break its grip—and doing so should be your first management procedure. Stop the bleeding with direct pressure and, afterward, thoroughly clean the bite wound. Splint the wounded area and find a doctor; nothing else of importance need be noted here.

### Important Note

Gila monsters freed from attachment to a victim have immediately turned the rescuer into a second victim.

# REPTILES OF OTHER NATIONS

Every year, worldwide, snakes kill more humans than does any other animal. Outside the United States, in climes as warm and warmer, you can find extremely dangerous snakes, especially members of the family Elapidae: the mambas, the cobras, the deadly elapids of Australia. The rough-scaled snake of Australia has killed an adult human within 30 minutes of the bite. The small-scaled (or fierce) snake of Australia has what most experts agree is the most potent venom in the world. Names such as death adder, gaboon viper, Malayan krait, bushmaster, and boomslang strike fear into many hearts. Venomous snakes even swim some of the Earth's seas, never found on land.

### A Closer Look: Potency of Snake Venom

The taipan of Australia carries a prodigious amount of venom, enough, state some experts, to kill 12,000 guinea pigs. The amount and potency of the venom of the king cobra of India is enough, say some experts, to kill an elephant. Snake venom may be rated according to the amount required to provide a lethal dose (LD) to 1 kilogram (32.15 ounces) of mice.

Small-scaled (fierce) snake venom LD =
0.01 milligram
Indian cobra venom LD = 0.50 milligram
American rattlesnake (average) venom LD
= 11.40 milligrams

## Treatment

Even though local customs may exist for managing bites in other nations, you need only apply the management principles for coral snake bites for elapids, and the principles for pit viper bites for other snakes. Unfortunately, your ultimate salvation after envenomization by some of the world's more potent snakes might well depend on the availability of anti-venin, and it is not always available in less developed countries. So watch your step!

## PREVENTION OF REPTILE BITES

- ✔ Do not try to pick up or otherwise try to capture snakes or lizards.
- ✔ Check places you intend to put your hands and feet before exposing your body part to a bite, especially in the dark.
- ✔ Gather firewood before dark, or do it carefully while using a flashlight.
- ✔ In snake country, keep your tent zipped up.
- ✔ Wear high, thick boots and/or gaiters while traveling in dangerous snake and lizard country.
- ✔ When passing a snake, stay out of striking range, which is about one-half the snake's length.
- ✔ If you hear the "buzz" of a rattler, freeze, find it with your eyes without moving your head, wait for it to relax its strike position, and back away slowly.

CHAPTER 2.

# *Dangerous Spiders*

> **IMAGINE THIS:**
> You hear cries of agony and rush to the tent to find a young
> woman in extreme discomfort, curled into a fetal position,
> complaining of severe cramps in her abdomen and lower
> back. Her pulse races, fast and weak, and a feverish sweat
> warms and cools her at once. Vomit splatters the tent walls.
> Thinking appendicitis, a rare and fatal gastroenteritis, or the
> imminent birth of an alien being, you are understandably dis-
> traught. On the other hand, maybe something bit her. How
> can you tell? What should you do?

An arachnid, as you know, has eight legs (four pairs). It also is a
member of the largest noninsect class of arthropods. An arachnid is not necessarily a spider—but this chapter is about spiders.
A few people know, and those who do not are seldom gladdened
to learn, that most spiders, worldwide, carry venom that can be
injected through nasty fangs. Furthermore, all spiders are carnivo-
rous and spend their lives waiting for and/or hunting for living
prey. Their venom is designed to paralyze their prey and liquefy
the tissues of the prey so the spider can then ingest the tissues.
Their venom in humans, then, causes predictable results: pain
and/or the death of local tissue.

On the positive side, only a few dozen species of spiders
on Earth have a bite harmful to humans. In the United States,
medical significance applies to only three types of spiders:
widows, browns, and hobos. Most spiders are harmless to
humans because they have a venom that does not work on
mammals, have too little venom to bother mammals, or have
fangs that cannot penetrate mammal, including human, skin.

Information relative to the precise statistical danger from spiders remains mysterious. A quote from the website of the Centers for Disease Control (CDC) is illustrative: "Venomous spider bites are not reportable in any state, and there are not reliable estimates of the incidences of such bites or how often medical attention is sought for them."

## A Closer Look: Jumping Spiders

Small, furry, crablike, and aggressive, the jumping spider (species *phidippus*) is rated by some experts as the North American spider most likely to bite. So aggressive is this spider that it sometimes bites without letting go. The victim walks into the emergency room with the spider still attached. Local reactions to the bite of the jumping spider include swelling and itching, with a dull pain that may last for days. Over-the-counter pain medications are usually effective, and long-lasting problems are rare.

## WIDOW SPIDERS

The widows (genus *Latrodectus*), of which there are at least five species common in North America, are spiders found around the globe. In the United States almost everyone is familiar with the black widow, an inhabitant of every state but Alaska. But one North American species of widow spider is brown, and one species is called the red-legged spider.

Only the females are dangerous to humans. The dark shiny female black widow, the one most often recognized, may reach about 2 inches (4–5 centimeters) in leg span, and she packs a remarkable potency in every little bit of venom. Drop for drop, widow venom is stronger than rattlesnake venom. Her venom's potential for harm makes her the most dangerous of spiders found in North America. The typically red—but not always red—hourglass shape on the underside of her abdomen helps identify her (see Figure 2.1). In some species, however, the two sides of the hourglass fail to meet, so you see two triangles almost joining. Males, by the way, are smaller (about one-third the size of females) and lighter in color, with even lighter markings and a faint hourglass. Males cannot bite through human skin.

**Figure 2.1 Black Widow Spider** *(underside view)*

The female widow spider secretes her tattered web under logs and large pieces of bark, in stone crevices, in trash heaps and outbuildings, and deep in clumps of heavy vegetation—and she infrequently leaves it. Rarely aggressive, she may be touchy during springtime mating and egg-tending days. Even then, she seldom bites unless she senses a threat to her web or a crushing presence against her body.

Even though their victims tend to fear they are dying, and then fear they will not die but live on in extreme pain, black widows kill very few humans. In the decade of the '60s, for instance, there were four confirmed fatalities from black widow bites. The dead are almost always the very young, the very old, or the very unhealthy. Many years, widow spiders of the United States claim no human lives.

### A Closer Look: The Widows

Many people believe widows derived their name from their predilection for killing and eating their mates. Those people are correct—but widows very often let their mates go without harming them. Some species of widows have been known to kill and eat small vertebrates such as lizards and snakes.

### Signs and Symptoms

Victims almost never feel the bite of the widow's sharp fangs, although some have reported immediate piercing pain. There may be little or no redness and swelling at the site initially, but a small, red, slightly hard bump may form later. Sometimes the bite site remains elusive, making a final diagnosis of spider bite difficult. Within 30 to 60 minutes, systemic symptoms may become disturbingly dramatic. Pain and anxiety become intense. Severe muscular cramping and rigidity often center in the large muscles of the abdomen, lower back, and limbs. Facial swelling may occur. Watch for headache, nausea, vomiting, dizziness, heavy sweating, and weakness—all common reactions. Weakness of the respiratory muscles has led to death.

### Treatment

Keep the victim as calm as possible—which is almost always a good thing to do for any victim for any reason. If you can find the bite site, wash it and apply an antiseptic such as povidone-iodine. Cooling the injury, with ice if possible or with water or wet compresses if necessary, will reduce the pain. Cold also reduces circulation, which slows down the spread of the venom. Medications for pain, if available, are appropriate. Strong medications for pain are often deeply appreciated by the victim.

Evacuation to a medical facility is strongly advised, especially if you are unsure what is causing the symptoms. People in severe pain are poor trail companions anyway. Most people will receive painkillers and muscle relaxers in the hospital, especially during the initial 8 to 12 hours when the agony tends to peak, and for one to three days of in-hospital observation. Youngsters, oldsters, and the very sick may be admitted for longer. Complete recovery can be expected, although pain may last for a week or more. Antivenin is available if needed.

## BROWN SPIDERS

The most common serious spider bite in the United States comes from a brown spider (genus *Loxosceles*), the most famous being *Loxosceles reclusa,* the true brown recluse spider. There are at least three other species in the United States, all members of the family Sicariidae, the recluse family. Some are called fiddlebacks and some violin spiders, and it really does not matter except to spider lovers. They almost all have the shape of a violin on the top front portion of their body. The head of this "fiddle" points toward the rear of the spider (see Figure 2.2). Generally they are colored pale brown to reddish, with long, slender legs about 1 inch (2–3 centimeters) in length. Both sexes of brown spiders, unlike the black widow, are dangerous.

### *Figure 2.2 Recluse Spider*

Brown spiders prefer the dark and dry places of the South and southern Midwest, but travel comfortably in the freight of trucks and trains, and probably can be found somewhere in all fifty states. In many states, however, it is rare to see a brown spider. They do not mind living near humans, and they will set up housekeeping underneath furniture, within hanging curtains, and in the shadowed corners of closets. In wildlands, they hide during the daylight hours beneath rocks, dead logs, and pieces of bark in forests. Solitary and "reclusive" of nature, they roam and hunt during the night. They bite more readily in the warmer months, usually at night, and only when threatened. Having relatively dull fangs, they tend to inflict wounds on tender areas of the human anatomy.

### Signs and Symptoms

Most humans bitten by a brown spider complain of sharp and stinging pain when the spider bites—although, as with many spiders, the bite can be painless and the victim unaware. Initial pain eases off, usually within 8 hours, to leave aching and perhaps itching as a replacement. A painful red blister appears where the fangs injected venom. Watch for the development of a bluish circle around the blister and a red, irritated circle beyond that—the characteristic "bull's-eye" lesion of the brown spider. The victim may suffer chills, fever, a generalized weakness, and a diffuse rash.

Sometimes the lesion resolves harmlessly over the next week or two. Sometimes it spreads irregularly as an enzyme in the spider's venom destroys the cells of the victim's skin and subcutaneous fat. Then the ulcerous tissue, the "volcanic" lesion, heals slowly and leaves a lasting scar. In a few children, death has occurred from severe complications in their circulatory systems.

### Treatment

As with many spider bites, the absence of an eight-legged corpse as evidence makes it difficult to be sure exactly what is causing the problem. Initially there is little to be done other than calming the victim and applying cold to the site of the bite for reduction of pain. The presence of systemic responses—such as fever and weakness—should initiate a quick trip to a doctor. "Volcanic" skin ulcers should also be seen by a physician as soon as possible. Antibiotic therapy usually cures the problem.

## HOBO SPIDERS

The hobo spider *(Tegenaria agrestis)* was accidentally imported from Europe, probably into Seattle and probably in the early 1900s. They have now spread across the northwestern United States, up into Alaska, and down into Utah. All hobo spiders are light brown, sometimes appearing to have a slightly green/yellow tint, with eight conspicuously hairy legs. The legs reach from 0.5 inch to 1.5 inches (1.25–3.75 centimeters). A herringbone stripe pattern in brown, gray, and/or tan often appears on the abdomen. Hobo spiders have been mistaken for brown spiders (the recluses) and are sometimes called Northwestern brown spiders. Hobos look like a recluse but lack the violin shape.

Some experts state the female hobo is more toxic, and some the male, but the dominant belief today is that the male is more toxic in terms of the necrotic (death) response in tissue. It is difficult to tell, and probably irrelevant, which sex you are looking at without special training and really keen eyesight.

Bites from hobo spiders are usually considered rare. Hobos tend to avoid large cities and congregate in small towns and rural communities. They like it under houses and deep in woodpiles and clumps of debris. Indoors they may lurk anyplace that is not regularly cleaned. It would be most unusual to find one out in the far, untrammeled places of the wilderness. They do not bite unless trapped against the skin of an unsuspecting human with no way to escape. Studies of hobo spider venom have been controversial and limited. Tests on rabbits show clear evidence of systemic poisoning from *Tegenaria* venom.

### Signs and Symptoms

In approximately 50 percent of human victims, it seems as if the bite of a hobo spider produces a lesion that ulcerates. It looks like the lesion of a *Loxosceles* bite, and often no one ever knows for sure which spider bit. Visual disturbances and/or disorientation in victims have been blamed on hobo spider venom, but the most common complaints are headache, muscle weakness, and lethargy.

### Treatment

No specific treatment has ever been developed for hobo spider bites. Follow the general guidelines for the management of brown spider bites described above.

## TARANTULAS

Due to a fierce appearance and perhaps even more fierce reputation (which is entirely undeserved), North American tarantulas (family Theraphosidae) are given a few words here. The most important words are these: They are relatively harmless. Some South American tarantulas, you may wish to note, are much more venomous—but, still, there are no known human deaths from their bites. Several species of tarantulas, including some of the ones in North America, have unusual and specialized barbed hairs that can be left in human skin.

### Signs and Symptoms

Pain, usually mild, seldom more than moderate, typically follows the tarantula's bite. Later signs and symptoms, such as weakness or collapse of the human victim, are rare, but they are cause for a physician's attention. The barbed hairs cause itchy bumps that may be bothersome for weeks.

### Treatment

Care for the bite as for any wound by washing and dressing it. Cold and/or medications for pain are appropriate treatment. The barbed hairs can—and should—be removed with any sticky tape. Topical anti-itch medications could be helpful.

## SPIDERS OF OTHER NATIONS

There are spiders more dangerous than the ones found in the United States. Of prime importance are Australia's funnel-web spiders, ranked by many experts as the world's most venomous arachnids. The Sydney funnel-web spider arguably holds top spot as the world's deadliest spider, having killed a human in less than 2 hours. Other fatalities from funnel-web spider bites are well documented. As with other types of venomous bites, small children are especially at risk after being bitten. Even so, human deaths are not common.

### Treatment

Worldwide, the backbone of treatment for spider bites is supportive care: Clean and manage any wound, give the victim painkillers as needed, and keep the victim hydrated. Funnel-web spider bites should be treated immediately with the pressure-immobilization technique described in the section on coral snakes in Chapter 1, Dangerous Reptiles. Antivenins to specific non–North American spider venoms often have been developed and may be available.

## PREVENTION OF SPIDER BITES

✔ Do not try to pick up or capture spiders.
✔ Check places you intend to put your hands and feet before exposing your body part to a bite.
✔ Gather firewood before dark, or do it carefully while using a flashlight.
✔ In dangerous spider country, keep your tent zipped up.
✔ If you must move around in the dark, wear boots or camp shoes.
✔ Take a look in your boots before putting them on in the morning.

CHAPTER 3.

# *Dangerous Scorpions*

> ***IMAGINE THIS:***
> *In the darkness in southern Utah, you feel the unpleasant tickle of something relatively large crawling on your exposed left arm, just above the elbow. You reach instinctively with a quick flick of your hand to brush away whatever it is. Fiery pain erupts immediately in the palm of your hand as a scorpion scuttles off rapidly into the night. What is going to happen to you? What are you going to do?*

Although experts disagree on the number of species of scorpions, they agree that at least thirty species, all in the family Buthidae, carry venom that can kill a human. From small ones that reach maturity at 0.75 inch to humongus 9-inchers, all scorpions have a somewhat lobsterlike appearance with four pairs of legs (making them arachnids) and a pair of pincers with which they grab their prey. Insects are their primary source of food, but some species will kill and devour small lizards. In all cases, they consume the juices and liquefied tissues of their prey, discarding the solid parts. They inhabit terrain, worldwide, where the temperature stays fairly warm.

Loving the night and hiding by day, some scorpions might be able to bite, but that fact is completely insignificant. Significant is the sting they are capable of delivering with the tip of their "tail" by arching it over their back. A scorpion's tail is actually an extension of the abdomen, and both stinger and venom glands reside in this tail.

**Fascinating Facts**

Uniquely, all scorpions glow when illuminated by ultraviolet light, such as a black light.

## BARK SCORPIONS

In the United States, where about forty scorpion species reside, only *Centruroides exilicauda*—sometimes called the bark scorpion—packs a wallop with potential for human death. Found throughout Arizona, bark scorpions are also seen in Texas, New Mexico, and, to a much lesser degree, parts of California and Nevada. No more than about 2 inches (around 5 centimeters) in length, they are a lean scorpion, described sometimes as "streamlined," with slender pincers (see Figure 3.1). Sometimes colored uniformly tan or brown, they probably appear yellowish most often.

*Figure 3.1 Centruroides Scorpion*

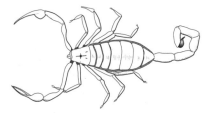

Between the years 1929 and 1954, in Arizona, where *Centruroides* stings are decidedly most common, there were sixty-nine deaths reportedly due to bark scorpion stings. Despite the possible complications, in Arizona the last confirmed human death by scorpion was in 1968.

### Signs and Symptoms

Most victims of any U.S. scorpion sting report no more pain than from an irritated honeybee sting. An attack of the species *Centruroides* may be different. The sting, immediately and exquisitely painful, is increased a lot by a light tap on the site. If the scorpion that stung was *Centruroides,* post-sting manifestations may include tingling in the extremities, heavy sweating, difficulty swallowing, blurred vision, loss of bowel control, and jerky muscular reflexes. The victim may writhe uncontrollably. Respiratory distress, and death, is possible.

The really bad things that can happen after a *Centruroides* sting typically peak at about 5 hours after envenomization. With small children, especially infants, the symptoms can be raging in as little as 15 minutes, and small children, as always, are at much greater risk for a serious reaction.

### Treatment

Even though scorpion envenomizations have long been known about and dealt with, very little specific treatment has been studied. First aid for any scorpion sting may involve cooling the wound, which may allow the body to more easily break down the molecular structure of the venom. Cooling also reduces pain. Use ice or cool running water if available. On a warm night, a wet compress helps. Keep the victim calm and still. Panic and activity speed up the venom's spread.

Systemic reactions to a *Centruroides* sting are cause for quick evacuation to a medical facility, but even then the standard care provided is supportive: painkillers, fluids, maintenance of normal body temperature, and such. Almost all victims notice marked improvement in 9 to 30 hours, although pain and tingling have persisted for as long as two weeks. Antivenin is available but usually withheld in the absence of very serious complications, and many experts consider its use controversial at best.

## SCORPIONS OF OTHER NATIONS
In some areas of the planet, scorpion stings pose a very serious and ever-present risk to humans. One estimate places the number of deaths worldwide at around 5000 per year, a fact that makes scorpions the second leading source of fatalities by animals, snakes holding down first place. Several species of the genus *Centruroides* may cause more than 400 deaths per year in Mexico, where definitive medical care is not available. Some experts guess that Mexican scorpions kill ten times more humans than do Mexican snakes.

South America and the Caribbean also shelter a few dangerous species. The genus *Tityus* in Brazil, for instance, currently carries a human kill rate of approximately 0.28 percent for all stings. Two to 3 percent of those people stung by the species *Mesobuthus tamulus,* India's only dangerous scorpion, die. Fatal scorpion stings are not unknown in the Near East, where in Saudi Arabia, for example, stings kill an estimated 2 to 5 percent of those stung. Every year, hundreds of humans die from scorpion stings in North Africa, where many thousands of people are stung by several very dangerous species.

### Treatment

Sometimes, in some of these areas, antivenin is available, and sometimes it works. In all areas, supportive care of the victim, as described above, should be provided. In most cases supportive care is enough.

## PREVENTION OF SCORPION STINGS

- ✔ Do not try to pick up or capture scorpions.
- ✔ Check places where you intend to put your hands and feet before exposing your body part to a sting.
- ✔ Gather firewood before dark, or do it carefully while using a flashlight.
- ✔ In scorpion country, keep your tent zipped up.
- ✔ If you must move around in the dark, wear boots or camp shoes.
- ✔ Take a look in your boots and shake out your clothing, places where scorpions like to hide, before dressing.

CHAPTER 4.

# *Ticks*

> **IMAGINE THIS:**
> *Your neck is stiff and other muscles ache. You have a low fever and unusual fatigue. All things considered, you feel crummy, as bad as you did with some kind of flu last year. But the frightening thing about this illness is the red rash that keeps appearing, growing, and fading—and the rash causes you pain. Should you find a doctor?*

With eight legs, ticks, like spiders and scorpions, are arachnids. Ticks are either hard bodied—family Ixodidae (see Figure 4.1)—or soft bodied—family Argasidae (see Figure 4.2). Ixodid ticks have three feeding stages of life—larval, nymph, and adult—and they almost always drop off their host in between feedings. They will feed on just about anything with blood—mammals, reptiles, and birds.

Unlike spiders and scorpions, ticks pass diseases to humans. Only mosquitoes, worldwide, transmit diseases more often to humans—and ticks pass a greater variety of diseases. In the

**Figure 4.1 Ixodid Tick**     **Figure 4.2 Argasid Tick**

United States, ticks are way ahead of mosquitoes in making humans sick. Though ticks can create a wound when they attach to a human, and though some can secrete a venom, their greatest risks to humans are not from wounds or venom but from the diseases they carry. If you get sick from a tick in North America, you got bit by an ixodid tick, with one exception: Argasid ticks carry relapsing fever.

After finding a host, a tick may search for hours before choosing a spot to settle down and eat. With specialized pincer-like organs, the tick digs a small, painless wound in the host. Into the wound goes a feeding apparatus called a hypostome, and a relatively powerful sucking mechanism allows the tick to then ingest the blood of the host. Anchored firmly in the wound, the tick feeds for an average of two to five days, and some-times longer than five days, depending on the species. If a tick picks up germs from one host, it will pass these germs to its next host—but following tick attachment, transmission of infection is frequently delayed, sometimes for more than 24 hours. Early meticulous examination for embedded ticks is mandatory, both diagnostically and therapeutically.

### A Closer Look: The Eating Habits of Ticks

Most adult ticks consume a single blood meal during their lives. Females must be engorged on blood to lay their eggs. They will gain up to fifty times their body weight while engorging.

## TICK REMOVAL

All ticks should be removed from the host as soon as they are found. While they are still free ranging, ticks can, of course, be easily removed.

Once ticks are attached, there is no known simple, effective, approved method of causing the tick to detach itself. The best method of tick removal—and the only Centers for Disease Control-approved method—is to gently grasp the animal with sharp-tipped tweezers as close as possible to the point of attachment, and remove by applying gentle traction. Grasp the tick perpendicular to its longitudinal axis. Grasping along its axis may turn the tick into a syringe, squirting its germy contents into the victim. Do not twist the tick. Do not jerk the tick. With slow, gentle traction, it is virtually impossible to tear off the tick's "head." A small piece of skin may come off painlessly with the tick, which almost always means tick removal is complete. Every effort should be made to avoid crushing the tick and contaminating either victim or helper with crushed tick material.

### Wound Treatment

After the tick is removed, the wound should then be cleansed with soap and water or povidone-iodine, and an adhesive strip bandage should be applied. Tweezers should be disinfected after use. If possible, the tick should be preserved for later identification in case the victim gets sick.

## TICK ENVENOMIZATION

Some ticks secrete toxins or venoms that, on one end of the clinical spectrum, cause a relatively mild local reaction. Pajaroello ticks (genus *Ornithodoros*), for instance, are greatly feared for their poison in some locales, but the bite is rarely serious. On the other end of the spectrum is tick paralysis (tick toxicosis), which results from a venom secreted in the saliva of at least forty-three species of ticks, some ixodids and some argasids. It occurs most often in the Pacific Northwest and the Rocky Mountains. The victim may develop serious complications and even die.

### Signs and Symptoms

Mild local reactions range from an itchy bump to a rather large red area. Tick paralysis begins with leg weakness, usually three days or so after the offending tick has attached. An ascending, flaccid paralysis follows, which progressively worsens as long as the tick is attached to the victim (usually a child). Speech dysfunction and difficulty swallowing are late signs, and death from aspiration or respiratory paralysis may occur.

### Treatment

For mild local reactions, if the wound from any tick bite will not heal, find a doctor. For tick paralysis, removal of the tick results in a progressive return to normal neurologic function.

## TICK-BORNE DISEASES

In the United States, eight tick-borne illnesses are considered indigenous, including the tick paralysis described above. The other seven diseases are listed below in alphabetical order.

### Babesiosis

Tick-transmitted protozoan parasites of the genus *Babesia* cause the disease babesiosis, a malarial-type illness. Although it is on the rise in the United States, most cases, but not all, have been limited to southern New England.

#### Signs and Symptoms

Typically the patient suffers a slow onset of fatigue, general malaise, and loss of appetite. A few days to a week or so later, fever, sweats, and achy muscles are common.

#### Treatment

Most people recover without any specific therapy, but unusual fatigue may hang on for much longer than anyone appreciates.

## Colorado Tick Fever

This disease is an acute, benign viral infection that occurs throughout the Rocky Mountain area during spring and summer.

### Signs and Symptoms

It is characterized by a sudden onset of fever followed by muscle aches, severe headache, loss of appetite, nausea, vomiting, and lethargy.

### Treatment

There is no specific therapy. The victim suffers until the disease runs its course.

## Erhlichiosis

Humans may get two forms of erhlichiosis: human monocytic erhlichiosis (HME) and human granulocytic erhlichiosis (HGE). Infected ticks must feed for a minimum of around 36 hours to pass enough of the bacteria that cause the illnesses.

### Signs and Symptoms

The flulike condition is characterized, in both HME and HGE, by a persistently high fever, headache, muscle aches, and joint pain. Rashes sometimes occur, more commonly with HME. Although most patients recover after a depressing monthlong illness, the percentage of people who die is almost as high as with Rocky Mountain spotted fever (see below), especially in the elderly and/or immunocompromised.

### Treatment

Antibiotics usually cure the victim of the disease.

## Lyme Disease

Lyme disease is a recently recognized inflammatory illness caused by *Borrelia burgdorferi* bacteria. As of 2002, Lyme disease accounts for approximately 90 percent of tick-borne illnesses in the United States, and the number of cases is on the rise. Areas of high risk are the Northeast, the upper Midwest, California, southern Oregon, and western Nevada. Most cases develop between early May and the end of November. It takes more than 24 hours of attachment for the tick to pass enough bacteria to cause the disease. Early removal means no illness.

### Signs and Symptoms
The first abnormality is far more often than not (occurring in 60 to 80 percent of cases) an expanding, well-defined red rash. The rash migrates: It fades from one area to appear in another. There is no relationship between where the tick bit and where the rash appears. Flulike symptoms often develop shortly after the rash appears and even if the rash fails to appear.

If untreated, months after the initial infection arthritis may develop, usually affecting the knees and shoulders. Persistent and varied neurologic abnormalities may occur and persist for years.

### Treatment
Medications shorten the duration of Lyme disease once it is established, and often prevent later problems.

## Relapsing Fever
Relapsing fever is an acute febrile illness caused by *Borrelia* bacteria of several species related to the one that causes Lyme disease. Infected ticks previously attached to wild rodents are the prime vectors for this disease.

### Signs and Symptoms
Clinically, initial symptoms are those of an acute flulike illness, but bouts continue at weekly intervals. The diagnosis is established by identification of the organism in blood smears.

### Treatment
Antibiotics knock the germs down for good.

### Prevention
Prophylactically, one should avoid staying in rodent-infested areas, especially in old abandoned cabins.

## Rocky Mountain Spotted Fever

In many areas of the United States—especially Montana, Oklahoma, Missouri, and the Carolinas—ticks can transmit a unique bacteria of the genus *Rickettsia,* causing Rocky Mountain spotted fever (RMSF). As recently as 1992, RMSF killed 5.2 percent of those infected. It is indeed the most fatal tick-borne disease in the United States.

### Signs and Symptoms

RMSF is an illness characterized initially by fever, headache, sensitivity to bright light, and muscle aches. On the third to fourth day of fever, a pink rash usually appears and may cover a large percentage of the victim's body.

### Treatment

If it is not treated promptly with antibiotics, the disease may be lethal.

## Tularemia

Since 1967, fewer than 200 cases per year of tularemia have been diagnosed in the United States. Though certainly it was once a disease associated with unhealthy contact with rabbits, ticks are now, by far, considered the prime transmission mode for the bacteria. Although many species of ticks have been incriminated, dog ticks and lone star ticks rank as the most common reservoirs. Rabbits still qualify as the second most common vector, but you must handle infected tissue, as you might do by skinning and eviscerating the little bunny. Wearing rubber gloves prevents transmission. You can also, very rarely, pick the disease up in water or soil by direct contact, ingestion, or breathing in contaminated dust or water particles.

### Signs and Symptoms

About 80 percent of tularemia cases appear as red bumps that harden and ulcerate, usually on the lower extremities where the tick bit. Ulcers are typically painful and tender. Enlarged, tender lymph nodes are common. The second most common form of tularemia, the typhoidal form, causes fever, chills, and debility. Weight loss may be significant. Pneumonia is a relatively common complication of tularemia.

*Treatment*

The treatment of choice is antibiotics.

## PREVENTION OF TICK BITES

✔ Wear light-colored clothing—the tick seen early is the tick picked off before it finds your skin—and wear long-sleeved shirts and long pants tucked inside a pair of high socks.

✔ Apply a permethrin-based tick repellent (actually an insecticide) to clothing prior to exposure, with particular attention to the ends of shirt sleeves and pants and about the collar area.

✔ Apply a repellent containing DEET (a concentration of no greater than 30 percent is recommended) to exposed areas of skin.

✔ Avoid contact with tall grass and brush whenever possible.

✔ Do not camp in places where you know ticks are running rampant.

✔ Perform twice-daily (morning and evening), full-body inspection for ticks—and immediately remove all free-ranging and embedded ticks.

CHAPTER 5.

# *Mosquitoes*

> **IMAGINE THIS:**
> *Your tent's mosquito netting stands stoutly between you and the buzzing of nocturnal predators. The odor of DEET permeates your daily life on the trail. Still, a few persistent skeeters find a place to bite. No big deal—or is it? What about all those mosquito-borne diseases America is dying from? Are you at risk?*

Of the phylum Arthropoda, no creature has a more significant impact on human beings than the mosquito, the most famous blood-sucking arthropod. Arguably, no other nonhuman life form has had as great an impact as mosquitoes. Their bites may sting and later itch, but the really bad news is this: When a mosquito sucks out your blood, it may leave disease-causing germs behind. Sure, they are bothersome, but consider this: Experts estimate than more than 700 million people will contract one of the nine known mosquito-borne diseases in the next year, and one of every seventeen humans currently alive will die because of a mosquito bite—not the bite, but the disease passed by the bite.

Only the female mosquito, requiring a blood feast in order to produce eggs, bites. She consumes up to her body weight with each meal, feeding once every three to four days. If you are the food source, she first probably "sees" you. Closer in, she "smells" you—carbon dioxide and lactic acid being studied as highly likely attractants. Your heat and body moisture are the final, irresistible lures. Male mosquitoes, in case you wonder, are vegetarians.

**Fascinating Facts**

✔ Mosquitoes bite men more often than they bite women.

✔ Mosquitoes bite adults more often than they bite children.

✔ Mosquitoes bite overweight people more often than they bite slim people.

## TREATMENT OF MOSQUITO BITES

Topical anti-itch products will work to reduce the discomfort of mosquito bites. If the product contains benzocaine, it will also provide pain relief. Steroid creams have little or no effect.

Oral antihistamines, available over the counter, reduce the itching.

Bites that have been scratched open should be washed and then monitored for signs of infection: increasing redness and swelling, increasing pain, red streaks appearing just beneath the skin.

**Fascinating Facts**

The following mosquito-borne diseases of the world are listed in alphabetical order.

Chikungunya fever
dengue fever
encephalitis (Eastern,
    Japanese, La Crosse,
    St. Louis, Western,
    Venezuelan varieties)

filariasis
malaria
Rift Valley fever
Ross River virus
West Nile virus
yellow fever

## MOSQUITO-BORNE DISEASES

Although mosquito-borne diseases have for many years been considered of little consequence to residents who do not leave the United States to travel to tropical and subtropical climates, that belief has been changing. True, the risk to the nontraveler remains very small, but a few diseases are worth knowing about.

### Dengue Fever

Dengue fever ranks as the most important viral disease on Earth passed by mosquitoes to humans, with a global distribution comparable to that of malaria (see below). An estimated total of 100 million cases of dengue will occur this year. Between 100 and 200 cases will be reported in the United States.

The female *Aedes aegypti* mosquito feeds during daylight hours, particularly in early morning and at twilight, and passes the disease to humans. She breeds not in swampy hinterlands but in the water-trapping refuse of humanity: discarded tires, plastic buckets, bottles, barrels, and cans.

#### Signs and Symptoms

If someone is bitten by a dengue-carrying mosquito, suddenly the victim's temperature shoots up as high as 104 degrees Fahrenheit, and a crushing headache makes the victim wonder whether a human skull can cave in from pain alone. The pain escalates behind the eyes when the victim looks right or left. Joints and muscles begin to ache, and nausea leads to vomiting. Three to four days later, a pale pinkish rash appears that spreads over the torso, out to the arms and legs, and up to the face. There exists an "empowered" form of dengue that often causes death, especially in small children. Most cases of dengue fever, however, last approximately seven to ten days, followed by a full recovery.

#### Treatment

The disease simply runs its course.

### Prevention

No vaccination is currently available, but work is proceeding on a promising candidate vaccine. As of 2002, if you are waiting for a shot to prevent dengue, you will be sitting around for five to ten years.

## Malaria

Somewhere between approximately 300 million and 500 million cases of malaria worldwide will cause as many as 3 million human deaths this year. A child dies of malaria every 30 seconds. Malaria is a huge health risk to people in tropical regions where the disease exists, and a great risk to travelers who visit those areas. In the United States, about 1,000 cases are reported annually.

This potentially fatal, severe febrile illness was once thought to result from breathing "swamp gas," the moist fumes rising from wet areas—the word *malaria* literally means "bad air." But all four species of the parasite (genus *Plasmodium*) causing the disease get into human blood only from the bite of the female *Anopheles* mosquito. The mosquito bites a sick person, picks up the parasites, then bites a healthy person, leaving some of the parasites behind.

### Signs and Symptoms

Typically, one to three weeks pass after the mosquito bites before signs and symptoms of malaria appear—but a year may pass before a victim knows that he or she is sick with *P. vivax* malaria. Malaria is famous for being difficult to diagnose, but all forms usually start with several days of fever and flulike symptoms: chills, headache, muscle aches. Sometimes stomach pain with vomiting and/or diarrhea make the victim think it is a gastrointestinal illness.

### Treatment

Anyone who has traveled to areas where malaria exists and who develops an unexplained fever should have his or her blood tested to determine whether he or she has malaria. If you think there is any chance you could have malaria, consult a physician as soon as possible.

### Prevention

*Anopheles* mosquitoes are primarily dusk and nighttime feeders. All precautions to prevent mosquitoes from biting (see Prevention of Mosquito Bites at the end of this chapter) should be taken when an *Anopheles* mosquito might bite. Unfortunately, the most ardent preventive steps can fail.

To be as safe as possible, travelers (with an agreeable doctor) may resort to chemical prophylaxis. The drug of choice for prevention of malaria has long been chloroquine—and it still is in many regions of the world—but some parasites have developed a resistance to it. In March 1990, the Centers for Disease Control (CDC) made mefloquine the officially approved prophylactic drug in chloroquine-resistant areas.

### A Closer Look: Four Species of Malaria

✔ *Plasmodium faciparum:* Found worldwide. Untreated victims often deteriorate rapidly and die.

✔ *Plasmodium malariae:* Found worldwide. May persist for years with few signs and symptoms in untreated victims. Rarely fatal.

✔ *Plasmodium ovale:* Relatively uncommon form found in western Africa. Rarely fatal.

✔ *Plasmodium vivax:* Found worldwide. Rarely fatal.

## West Nile Virus

In Uganda in 1937, the first case of West Nile virus was officially identified, but no known case appeared in the United
States until the summer of 1999. Since that first victim in the
New York City area, the disease has been reported in thirty-
five states in the Northeast, South, and Midwest, and may have
reached, as of August 2002, as far west as Colorado.

As of September 2002, there have been more than forty
confirmed deaths due to West Nile virus in the United States.
The chances of death are greater by far for people who are
more than fifty years old and/or immunocompromised. Less
than 1 percent of the people in the United States who have
been proven to have the disease have died.

Mosquitoes seem to get the virus from infected birds and
maintain it in their salivary glands—then spread it to humans
when the insects bite and feed. As of August 2002, less than
1 percent of mosquitoes in virus-prevalent areas carry the disease. West Nile virus has also been found in horses, cats, bats,
chipmunks, squirrels, skunks, and domestic rabbits, but there
is no evidence that humans get the virus from those animals
without a mosquito serving as the go-between. There is
no evidence that any other arthropod can pass the disease.
Humans cannot pass the disease to other humans.

### Fascinating Facts

Your chances of being struck by lightning are slightly
better than your chances of dying of the West Nile virus.

### Signs and Symptoms

Although West Nile virus is spreading rapidly across the United
States and cases in humans are definitely on the rise, fewer

than one in five people who contract the disease develop any symptoms. If the signs and symptoms develop, it takes three to fourteen days (five to fifteen days, say some experts) after the victim is bitten, and they are almost always mild and flulike, including fever, headache, muscle aches, and, occasionally, a rash on the trunk of the body and swollen lymph glands. These signs and symptoms eventually go away harmlessly, usually within a few days.

In rare cases, however—approximately 1 in 150—the virus can cross the blood-brain barrier and cause a serious inflammation of the brain (known as West Nile encephalitis), a serious inflammation of the membranes surrounding the brain and the spinal cord (known as West Nile meningitis), or a serious inflammation of the brain and its surrounding membranes (known as West Nile meningoencephalitis). Serious signs and symptoms may include headache, high fever, neck stiffness, stupor, disorientation, coma, tremors, convulsions, muscle weakness, and paralysis. In severe cases, problems may persist for weeks, and neurological effects may be permanent.

### Treatment

Travelers who have been in an area where West Nile virus could be carried by mosquitoes, who have been bitten by mosquitoes, and who think they could have the virus should see a physician as soon as possible. A blood test can confirm the presence of the disease. Unfortunately, there exists no specific treatment for West Nile virus, but supportive care leads to a complete recovery in all but 3 to 15 percent of severe cases. And once a person gets West Nile virus, the victim probably can never get it again.

### Prevention

To date, no vaccine has been developed for West Nile virus. Research is ongoing, but estimates place success years down the trail.

### Important Note

For updates on West Nile virus and other diseases transmitted by bite or sting, call the Centers for Disease Control toll-free 24 hours a day at 888-232-3228, or go to their website at *www.cdc.gov*.

### A Closer Look: Permethrin

Permethrin, originally extracted from chrysanthemum flowers, is a potent insect neurotoxin currently synthesized for human use as an insect repellent. Not really a repellent, permethrin is an insecticide—an insect killer. Within minutes after contact with permethrin-treated clothing, the insect dies. It kills mosquitoes, ticks, fleas, flies, lice, and mites. It bonds strongly to the fibers of clothing and, depending on the concentration and application process, can withstand numerous washings, remaining active, in some cases, for years. Permethrin is colorless and odorless, and does no harm to vinyl, plastic, or other fabrics. It can be applied to mosquito netting on tents, to sleeping bags, even to window screens at home. It should not be applied to human skin. After many tests, experts agree that it apparently does no harm to humans, but it does not work as a repellent or insecticide when applied to skin.

## PREVENTION OF MOSQUITO BITES

✔    Wear clothing thick enough or tightly woven enough to prevent penetration of the mosquito's biting apparatus. Wear long sleeves and long pants to reduce the skin mosquitoes have access to. Wear light-colored clothing: khaki, etc. Mosquitoes seem to be partial to dark colors, especially blue.

✔    Apply permethrin, a safe insecticide, to clothing (see sidebar).

✔    Apply an insect repellent to exposed skin.

✔    Sleep under mosquito netting or inside tents with mosquito netting.

✔    Avoid exposure during prime mosquito-biting time, usually dawn and dusk.

✔    Avoid mosquito-prone areas: near standing water, dense vegetation, and areas known to be thick with mosquitoes.

### Comparing Repellents

A study reported in the *New England Journal of Medicine* in 2002 confirmed that nothing repels better than DEET (see below). Repellents containing 23.8 percent DEET kept bugs away for a mean complete-protection time of 301.5 minutes (5 hours). In the *Journal* report, products containing lemon eucalyptus worked second best, repelling bugs for a mean complete-protection time of 120.1 minutes (2 hours). Third place went to a product containing soybean oil that repelled mosquitoes for a mean complete-protection time of 94.6 minutes (1.6 hours). See Table 5.1, Protection Times of Insect Repellents, for additional comparisons.

### Table 5.1
### Protection Times of Insect Repellents

| Active Ingredient | Mean Complete-Protection Time |
| --- | --- |
| DEET, 23.8% | 301.5 +/- 37.6 minutes |
| DEET, 20% | 234.4 +/- 31.8 minutes |
| Lemon eucalyptus | 120.1 +/- 44.8 minutes |
| DEET, 6.65% | 112.4 +/- 20.3 minutes |
| Soybean oil, 2% | 94.6 +/- 42.0 minutes |
| DEET, 4.75% | 88.4 +/- 21.4 minutes |
| IR3535, 7.5% | 22.9 +/- 11.2 minutes |
| Citronella, 10% | 19.7 +/- 10.6 minutes |
| Bath oil | 9.6 +/- 8.8 minutes |

Source: New England Journal of Medicine 347, no. 1 (July 4, 2002)

### Fascinating Facts

Neither ultrasonic devices nor repelling wrist bands have proven to repel mosquitoes. Tests run with more than 100 drugs, including vitamin C, vitamin B1 (thiamine), and other vitamins failed to reveal that anything was repelled. The Food and Drug Administration has stated that all claims for products to repel insects if taken orally are "either false, misleading, or unsupported by scientific data."

## How to Use DEET-Based Repellents

Read the label carefully before use. Use a concentration of no more than 30 percent. Higher concentrations provide longer protection but *not* better protection. Apply repellent sparingly. Heavy application and saturation are unnecessary. Repeat applications only as necessary. Do not apply over cuts, wounds, or irritated skin, and keep it out of eyes and mouth. Discontinue if skin irritation develops.

Do not apply to children's hands or allow children to handle the product. Kids will smear the repellent into their eyes and mouths. No specific data relates to the use of DEET on children, but the American Academy of Pediatrics recommends a concentration of no more than 10 percent on children ages two to twelve years. Avoid use on children under two, say some experts, but others say DEET is OK on children under two if it is used no more than once a day.

After exposure ends, wash skin where DEET was applied—and give little kids a bath.

Avoid inhaling the aerosol and spray products that contain DEET.

Avoid getting DEET on plastic products. It may cause deterioration of the plastic.

## A Closer Look: DEET

Known as DEET—N, N-diethyl-m-toluamide, or more often now called N, N-diethyl-3-methylbenzamide—we can count ourselves fortunate that we only have to ask for it by the common name. Available since 1957, DEET has been applied to human skin more than an estimated eight billion times. In all those applications, fewer than fifty cases of serious toxic effects have been documented, and three-fourths of those cases resolved without permanent harm to the victim. Many of the toxic cases involved long-term and/or heavy use of DEET. No correlation between concentration of DEET and the risk of toxic effects has ever been found.

CHAPTER 6.

# *More Blood-Feeding Arthropods*

### *IMAGINE THIS:*
*Your campsite sits pleasantly near a prairie dog town. Ah, they are cute, are they not? Except for that dead one lying near where you decided to put up your tent—so you moved the little carcass away. Later you notice a really itchy set of bumps on your shoulder. Could they be related, the bumps and the prairie dogs? Should you be concerned?*

When the first humanoid crawled out of the first cave to greet the first prehistoric dawn, something with more legs than he or she had was waiting, something small and annoying that scurried or flew, something that punctured or drilled or excavated the humanoid's skin with total disregard for emerging human rights. These little creatures acted as if they owned the place, a justifiable act since they, in some form, had been here about 350 million years already. Regardless of who was right, humanoid or bug, one of the first uses of the human hand was probably to swat. Nothing much has changed in the wild outdoors.

If you take the total weight of all humans today, and the total weight of all life forms with six legs, you get approximately the same number—roughly eleven million tons. True insects all have six legs, but they are only a part of that vast multilegged group of beings (arthropods) that bug humans. History reads richly of human attempts to keep bugs off them, a story of utter desperation and failure—and sometimes of disease.

**Fascinating Facts**

Below are some of the diseases transmitted by some arthropods of the world.

Fleas: plague, murine typhus

Flies: tularemia, leishmaniasis, African trypanosomiasis, onchocerciasis, bartonellosis, loa loa

Lice: epidemic typhus, relapsing fever

Mites: scrub typhus, rickettsial pox

Sucking bugs: American trypanosomiasis

## FLEAS

Fleas (family Pulicidae) are wingless insects composed mostly of legs and mouth (see Figure 6.1). They can jump really high and bite really well. There are many species living on birds and mammals worldwide, some feeding on a particular host, some feeding indiscriminately on any host, all feeding on blood. Both sexes are blood-feeders and, unlike many arthropods, both will bite several times while feeding instead of the customary hit-and-run tactics of most insects.

Fleas are important to consider partly because their bites are uncomfortable and mostly because they can pass disease to humans, including several forms of plague. Carried by rodents and passed primarily by the bite of rodent fleas, the bacteria that causes plague also kills both rodent and flea, an unusual aspect of this disease. Black rats are especially suscep- tible, and *Rattus rattus* is blamed for the Black Death of the fourteenth century (see sidebar).

Since fleas will not leave a host until they have fed well, and since most travelers will not be near enough to many wild animals for their fleas to transfer to them, the chance of getting

### *Figure 6.1 Flea*

bitten by a plague-ridden flea is small. Most of the cases reported in recent years have been acquired by people who handled dead animals. Hikers and campers may be at mild risk if they hang around rodent-infested areas.

### A Closer Look: The Plague

Between A.D. 1347 and 1350, the Black Death, caused by the bacterium *Yersinia pestis,* began somewhere in Asia and eventually rubbed out about twenty-five million Europeans (roughly one-third the population). Nine-tenths of the people of England were permanently laid low. Before those devastating years, even in B.C. days, reports of the scourges of plague were known and feared.

### Flea-Borne Diseases: Plague

In recent years plague has been on the rise in the western United States, where deer mice and various voles maintain the bacteria. It is amplified in prairie dogs and ground squirrels. Other possible reservoirs include chipmunks, marmots, wood rats, rabbits, and hares. Coyotes and bobcats are known to have transmitted plague to humans after the critters were dead and the humans were skinning them. Skunks, raccoons, and badgers are also suspect in the skinning process. Meat-eating pets that eat infected rodents (or get bitten by infected fleas) can acquire plague. Dogs do not get very sick, but cats do. There is only one known case of plague being passed to a human by a dog, but several cats have passed the disease to several humans by biting them, coughing on them, or carrying their fleas to them. Sick people transmit plague readily to other people. Several forms of plague exist, but the three most common are bubonic, septicemic, and pneumonic.

**Bubonic plague** gets its name from buboes, inflamed, enlarged lymph nodes. After an incubation period of two to six days, patients usually suffer fever, chills, malaise, muscle aches, and headaches. Blackened, bleeding skin sores arise—thus the name "Black Death."

**Septicemic plague** may appear similar to bubonic plague but does not give rise to buboes; gastrointestinal pain with nausea, vomiting, and diarrhea are common.

**Pneumonic plague** results most often from inhaling droplets that contain the bacteria, but it can develop from bacteria that got into the victim's blood. With the pneumonic form, coughing often produces blood in the sputum.

### Signs and Symptoms

Flea bites tend to itch a lot, so much so that scratching removes the bumps and it may not be possible to be sure later that something bit the victim. If it is possible that a flea bit the victim and, within a week, the person develops a high fever, chills, headache, and muscle aches, it might be the plague—most commonly bubonic plague, similar to the Black Death that ravaged Europe long ago, but not as ravaging now.

### Treatment

If plague is suspected, it should be treated soon by a physician. Fatalities are common today, especially in the pneumonic and septicemic forms. The treatment drug of choice is often the antibiotic streptomycin, injected four times a day for five days.

### *Prevention*

Prevention includes avoidance of rodents and rodent-rich areas, avoiding touching sick or dead animals (if you must touch them, wear rubber gloves), restraining dogs and cats while traveling in infected areas (because they can pick up infected fleas), and using effective insect repellents (see Chapter 5, Mosquitoes).

## FLIES

Females of numerous species of the order Diptera (the two-winged flies) require blood (or sometimes other vertebrate fluids) to reproduce. Not true "biters" in the usual sense of the word, they have mouthparts evolved into efficient tools for stabbing and sucking. Many flies, therefore, are well equipped to be very effective nuisances. And since they feed on multiple hosts, they can also be effective transmitters of illnesses. Mosquitoes, for instance (see Chapter 5), fall into this order, but they have relatives worldwide that are almost as well known and disliked.

### A Closer Look: The Tsetse Fly

Only tropical Africa provides habitat for the tsetse fly (genus *Glossina*), a creature somewhat famous for transmitting to humans the disease African trypanosomiasis (sleeping sickness). Infected victims typically develop a fever, headache, and profound malaise that disappears, perhaps reappearing later with severe complications, including heart failure. A physician's care is required. Repellents that work on other flies work on the tsetse fly.

## Blackflies

These flies are small, broad-winged, humpbacked, and, of course, black. Unlike mosquitoes, which prefer still water, blackfly eggs hatch happily in flowing water, anything from large rivers to small streams, and they are most often encountered near moving water. Flying the thickest in late spring and early summer, their range is worldwide, extensive, and surprisingly far north. And thickly they may indeed fly, hatching in great swarms in some areas.

Like mosquitoes, blackflies (family Simuliidae) are initially attracted to a meal by visual stimulants, especially dark moving food sources. Body heat and carbon dioxide probably add more attraction. Blackflies seem capable of squirming down to skin, regardless of clothing worn and even using repellents, and enjoying a feast. Blackflies are arguably the most difficult of winged insects to avoid.

Also like mosquitoes, only the female bites and feeds on blood. She tears away a tiny bit of skin and sucks up the blood that pools in the wound. Unswatted, she may feed for up to 5 minutes. And you may not swat because the fly often causes no pain when she bites. Blood may continue to leak from the wound long after the fly has flown on to better things.

If there is something good to say about blackflies, and many people will argue heatedly that there is not, it could be this: There are no known diseases transmitted from blackflies to humans in North America. Unfortunately, tropical blackflies do pass germs that may cause illness in people.

### Signs and Symptoms

The wound becomes painful and severely itchy, and is notoriously slow to heal.

### Treatment

There is no specific treatment available.

### Figure 6.2 Tabanid Fly

## Deerflies and Horseflies

Of the family Tabanidae, deerflies and horseflies (and numerous related species around the world) are born in very wet soil or shallow water. Large, as flies go, they have an unusually strong flying ability that can carry them for miles. They are all darkish, but some have rather bright-colored eyes (see Figure 6.2). Only the females are attracted to blood meals, primarily by seeing movement of the meal. More a cut from scissorlike mouthparts than a bite, the resulting wound bleeds and the fly feeds.

### Signs and Symptoms

Sometimes quite painful, the bite of these flies is also usually intensely itchy and may bleed for a bit. On rare occasions the bites have produced a systemic reaction in victims, such as widespread itching and serious allergenic reactions. Tabanid bites have transmitted tularemia to humans in the United States (see Tick-Borne Diseases in Chapter 4, Ticks) and loa loa (a parasitic worm) to humans in Africa.

### Treatment

Some bites have led to a secondary infection, and therefore should be cleaned well. Systemic reactions should send the victim to a physician as soon as possible.

### Prevention

These flies are kept away by effective insect repellents.

## Midges

Small enough to be almost invisible at times, biting midges (family Culicoides) are small flies known by such names as "no-see-ums," "sand gnats," and, perhaps most appropriately, "flying teeth." Found worldwide, they breed in salt- and freshwater wetlands.

Midges have the annoying ability to squirm their small bodies through otherwise protective netting. Females are unusually aggressive, attacking sometimes in swarms. Some species attack during the night and some prefer the daylight. No midge is known to transmit disease to humans in North America.

### Signs and Symptoms

Midges leave numerous painful and itchy bites.

### Treatment

Treat the same as mosquito bites.

### Prevention

Effective insect repellents work to keep midges from biting.

## Sand Flies

Tropical and subtropical habitats may give rise to the little, hairy, long-legged sand fly (see Figure 6.3). Once again, only the females feed on blood, and they may pass several diseases, including bartonellosis and leishmaniasis. So far the only disease passed by a sand fly to a human in the United States is a form of leishmaniasis, an infection primarily affecting the

### *Figure 6.3 Sand Fly*

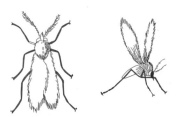

skin and upper airway. A doctor's care is required. So far it has occurred only in Texas.

**Prevention**
Effective insect repellents work on sand flies.

## LICE

Tiny and wingless, lice (order Anoplura) are parasitic insects that live on a host and feed on the blood of the host. Their mouthparts allow them to pierce and suck. Most of them prefer a specific host, and two species of lice live exclusively on humans. No lice are known to transmit diseases to humans.

**Pubic lice,** one of these species, prefer, you guessed it, the pubic region of the human body, where they find footholds in the hair. Somewhat crablike in appearance, you may hear this species referred to as crab lice or "crabs." They actually cement their nits (eggs) to the hair shafts, where they develop into adults in about fifteen days. With an average life expectancy of thirty-five days, during which time the female lays around three eggs per day, pubic lice are capable of hanging around indefinitely. They are passed easily from one host to another during intimate physical contact, but they may also be passed through infested clothing.

**Head lice and body lice,** two varieties of the other species, live in the hair on human heads, and in the seams of clothing, respectively. Body lice come out five or six times a day to feed. Contrary to their name, body lice are not found on the body except during periods of feeding. Head lice reach maturity in about ten days and the females may lay up to six eggs per day. They are smaller and less crablike than pubic lice. Both varieties are passed easily through close contact with infested persons' hair and/or clothing.

### Signs and Symptoms

All lice make themselves known by the same manifestation: itching. They cause so much itching that secondary infections from the scratching are not uncommon.

### Fascinating Facts

A single individual of a lice species is called a louse, a word used to describe a person (lousy) or a predicament (loused up).

### Treatment

All lice can be killed with appropriate medical treatment, which involves, in all cases, eradicating the nits as well as the bugs. Creams are available that usually work with one application—follow the directions on the label. Washing clothing in hot water kills lice and nits in clothing.

## MITES

Some so small they are barely visible to the naked eye, mites make up the largest group of the eight-legged, the class Arachnida, and they are found around the world. Of about 35,000 species of mites, approximately 50 species are known to cause skin reactions in human victims. Some of the skin reactions result from the mite feeding and some from the mite burrowing into the skin. Some mites pass diseases to humans.

### Fascinating Facts

Occasionally humans suffer delusions of parasitosis, convinced, despite all evidence to the contrary, that parasites inhabit their skin. Victims will claim to feel things crawling on their skin, with accompanying burning and/or stinging sensations. Psychiatric treatment, even antipsychotic drugs, are often unsuccessful, and the victims will scratch themselves into self-mutilated conditions.

### Chiggers

"A chigger, I figger, is a critter no bigger than the dot on the head of a pin," wrote an anonymous sufferer. But they are not even that big. You cannot usually see them, even though they are bright red mites (family Trombiculoid) and have eight legs (see Figure 6.4). Also known as red bugs and harvest mites, they hang out in swarms during their larval stage of life, on vegetation, usually close to the ground, waiting for a warm-blooded host. They usually seek a place on a human body where clothing fits snugly. Once finding a suitable spot, they break the victim's skin, release a saliva that liquefies epidermal cells, and feed for two to three days by sucking up the liquefied tissue. The saliva they release forms a tube behind them as they move along feeding.

#### Signs and Symptoms

During chiggers' feeding time, the victim itches with indescribable ferocity and scratches aggressively, often scratching off

### Figure 6.4 Chigger

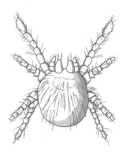

the offending mite. If left to reach satiation, chiggers fall off to grow toward adulthood. The tubes, filled with irritants to human skin, are left behind. The victim is left with small, reddened, fluid-filled bumps that itch miserably for another week or two.

### Treatment

Once the itching starts, topical anti-itch ointments provide some relief.

### Prevention

Other than avoiding chigger country, preventive measures include using insect repellents that keep mosquitoes off, which will usually keep these little beasties off as well.

## Scabies

Human scabies mites *(Sarcoptes scabiei)* range over the human body, living their entire lives, birth to death (a period of about thirty to sixty days for females), on and in the skin of people. The smaller males live brief lives mostly on the skin's surface, where they copulate and then die. Once the adult female gets pregnant, she burrows into the victim's skin and sleeps all day. At night she awakens, lays a few eggs, and burrows around some more while she feeds. The eggs hatch, and the larvae mature to adults to continue the life cycle, all on the same host. Being quite good at reproduction, scabies can persist indefinitely.

Usually transmitted from one human to another during intimate contact, scabies mites can live separated from a human for only about 24 to 36 hours. In the wild outdoors, they may be passed by sharing sleeping bags with or without the infected human being in the bag with the new victim.

### Signs and Symptoms
At night, when the female mite is feeding, is when the intense itching of scabies occurs. Itching may be intensified by heat, such as a warm bath. Sometimes the burrows in the skin are visible on careful examination.

### Treatment
Scabies is usually cured fairly rapidly with topical treatments such as a 5 percent concentration of permethrin cream.

## SUCKING BUGS
Of the order Hemiptera, sucking bugs most often suck up plant juices, but members of two families are eager to feed on the blood of humans.

### Assassin Bugs
The assassin bug, also known as the conenose bug or kissing bug, is so called for its tendency to bite near the mouth and/or on the lips. Both sexes are nocturnal blood-feeders, reaching about 1 inch (10–30 millimeters) in length at maturity, usually dark brown or black, with stubby wings and extended mouthparts (see Figure 6.5). Kissing bugs are poor fliers, preferring to sort of plop onto exposed skin from brush on dry hillsides and canyons, from hollow trees, and from under tree bark. Perhaps the origin of the name assassin bug is because they tend to leap onto you in the dark. They also love to rest

### *Figure 6.5 Assassin Bug*

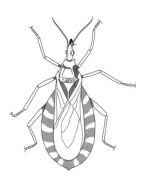

in palm trees and thatched roofs. They are found in the south-western United States, including Texas and California (and in many parts of Central and South America). Disgustingly, they defecate while they are feeding. Kissing bugs are the vector for Chagas' disease (American trypanosomiasis).

### Signs and Symptoms

If the victim wakes up with tiny, itchy wounds near the mouth or eyes after sleeping outdoors in the Southwest, these wounds have been left by the assassin bug's painless bite. If the victim wakes and rubs the places that itch, there is a high probability that the germ-ridden bug defecation will be smeared into the wound the bug has left, which is a means of disease transmission.

If a victim gets a red bump that soon fades, followed, in a week or so, by firm swelling and a fever, he or she better see a doctor. Chagas' disease appears to go away, but actually hangs around for years, slowly eats at the heart, and ends in premature death.

Chagas' disease aside, many people have a severe allergic reaction to the "kiss" of the assassin bug (see the Anaphylaxis section in Chapter 7, The Stinging Arthropods). Deaths are uncommon, but have been reported.

### Treatment
Treat the wounds by simply washing them. If Chagas' disease develops, it is curable with drugs.

### Prevention
When in the assassin bug's territory, sleep in a tent or under a mosquito net.

## Bedbugs
So called because they find homes in human dwellings, especially adobe buildings, and come out to join humans in bed at night, bedbugs (family Cemicidae) are small insects, reddish brown, and unable to fly. They feed on blood, attracted by its warmth. They usually have a painless bite. On the plus side, bedbugs are not known to transmit diseases to humans.

### Signs and Symptoms
Bedbugs typically leave a short line of red, itchy bumps where they recently fed. The bumps and the itch go away, often less quickly than most hosts wish.

### Treatment
Treatments do not work well. Topical anti-itch medications sometimes help with mild reactions. Heat applied to the bite sites sometimes helps with more severe reactions.

### Prevention
Keeping bedding clean is helpful. Bedbugs, however, are difficult to eradicate without insecticide use—and even then sometimes persist. Expert advice on eradication is recommended.

## PREVENTION OF BUG BITES

There are three ways to keep these arthropods from biting or sucking blood. To bug-proof your life on the trail, you can kill the bug, drive the bug away, or keep the bug from accessing your skin.

### Killing the Bug

Widespread use of insecticides is impractical at best on wilderness trips, and unkind to the environment at worst. Permethrin, however (see the sidebar in Chapter 5, Mosquitoes) applied to clothing and gear is an effective local insecticide.

### Driving the Bug Away

The ideal repellent is effective against all kinds of bugs, harmless to skin and clothing, and pleasing to the senses of humans—the ideal repellent, in other words, does not exist. Repellents that come close are discussed in the prevention section in Chapter 5, Mosquitoes.

### Keeping the Bug from Accessing Your Skin

Wear loose-fitting, tightly woven clothing of a light color. Tight-fitting clothing will allow some bugs, such as mosquitoes, to bite through to your skin. Wide-brimmed hats discourage many insects from investigating beneath. Head nets are worthy considerations in densely insect-inhabited areas. Tents should be checked to make sure the netting is intact.

## Additional Suggestions

✔ Before traveling in an area, gather specific information from local land managers and/or health officials about what insect-transmitted diseases might exist there and how to avoid them.

✔ Set up camp well away from wet areas and moving or standing water during bug season. Use open areas with little vegetation. Set up camp to take advantage of breezes that push away many bugs.

✔ Avoid lights at night as much as possible. Many bugs are attracted to light.

✔ Clean up thoroughly after meals, closing and storing anything that might attract bugs.

✔ Do not sleep with anything that might attract bugs or other animals: food, garbage, toothpaste, deodorant, soap, or other scented products. Choose unscented camp soap, lotion, toilet paper, etc.

✔ Keep your tent door zipped shut.

✔ Never approach or try to feed a live animal.

✔ Never touch a dead animal.

✔ Leave your pets at home—or, if you must take them along, keep them close and under control. They will bring bugs back to you.

CHAPTER 7.

# *The Stinging Arthropods*

### IMAGINE THIS:

*As you lifted a red bloom to your nose for a sniff, you did not notice the honeybee inside industriously gathering nectar. Startled, the bee responded in an appropriately beelike way: It stung you. The back of your hand hurts, but not unbearably, and a wheal starts to rise. No big deal, really, except suddenly you notice a tightness in your chest. Your breathing starts to require some effort. What is going on? What will you do?*

The stinging arthropods (order Hymenoptera) are widespread and related largely due to their habit of injecting venom when they sting. In all the hymenopterans, the biological wherewithal to manufacture, store, and inject their venom is situated in the most posterior section of their anatomy. In the United States, most honeybees are gold-colored, but a few may be seen of a second species that is black and gray. Along with the bumblebee and three species of social wasps (paper wasp, yellow jacket, and hornet) and fire ants, bees are the common stinging arthropods you will encounter. Other species, only occasionally seen, are beyond the scope of this book.

## Signs and Symptoms

When the hymenopterans sting, pain is immediate, redness and swelling soon follow, and itching may not be far behind. The pain may be described as intense, depending on the species that stung, with hornets often responsible for some of the worst pain. Most humans find the pain extremely annoying, and that is the end of the story. Some experience mild to moderate allergic reactions, characterized by hives, facial swelling, and dizziness.

### Anaphylaxis

A severe allergic reaction, in this case to the venom, is called anaphylaxis. Every year, an estimated 50 to 100 people in the United States die from a hymenopteran sting, usually in less than an hour, almost always the result of anaphylaxis. Some experts guess the fatality rate runs even higher.

*Anaphylaxis is a true, life-threatening emergency.* Breathing difficulties (from airway constriction) and/or anaphylactic shock (from rapidly dilating blood vessels) that result in a true anaphylactic reaction require rapid field treatment—or else the victim dies.

### Treatment

For a nonallergic reaction, the pain of a sting by a hymenopteran is diminished by immediately applying cold to the site. Some topical analgesics ease the pain. Antihistamines reduce both the duration and extent of the local reaction. Steroid creams may decrease the local reaction, but no topical medications have proven truly effective for reducing the reaction.

Mild to moderate allergic reactions can be treated with an oral antihistamine.

### Treating Anaphylaxis

If severe difficulty in breathing results, the ability to reverse fatal anaphylaxis requires the administration of epinephrine.

Inhaled epinephrine, a nonprescription drug, may relax the airway enough to be life-saving. Unfortunately, inhaled epinephrine will not work if the victim cannot inhale—plus it does little or nothing for shock.

The most specific and valuable treatment is the use of

injectable epinephrine, available by prescription in preloaded syringes in kit form. It works to alleviate both breathing difficulties and shock. Some physicians recommend that three total doses be carried at all times by people who know they are severely allergic, and some physicians recommend four doses or even more.

This is because sometimes one injection is not enough. A second injection should be given in 5 minutes if the condition of the victim worsens, and in 15 minutes if the condition of the victim does not improve. Rebound or recurrent reactions can occur up to 24 hours after the original incident.

As soon as the victim can breathe and swallow, an oral antihistamine should be given. Many over-the-counter antihistamines are available, with diphenhydramine currently being the most often recommended post-epinephrine treatment. The recommended dose of diphenhydramine is 50 to 100 milligrams to start, and approximately 50 milligrams every 4 to 6 hours until the victim is turned over to definitive medical care.

## BEES

Bee venom itself is not very toxic. It is not designed to kill but simply to repel threats. There is no difference in human reactions to stings from different types of bees, but as many as 15 percent of all humans may have some sensitivity, often mild, to bee venom.

Nonaggressive by nature, the honeybee, unlike all other stinging insects, has a barbed stinger that rips out of the insect and stays in human skin, continuing to pump venom for up to 20 minutes. Within a day or so of stinging, the bee dies. Interesting to note, honeybees are not native American, having been imported from Europe as domestic animals. They escaped and do nest in the wild. Stings in the wild, as in backyards, are accidental.

### *Figure 7.1 Honeybee's Barbed Stinger*

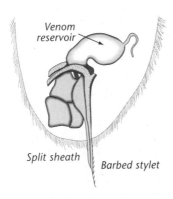

Honeybees lead the swarm as a source of fatalities in humans. Indeed there is no more potentially deadly animal in North America. It takes usually 40 to 50 simultaneous stings to cause a systemic reaction. It takes, depending on the individual who got stung, somewhere between about 500 and 1,400 simultaneous stings to cause death by toxicity.

Bumblebees, also toxic, grow to two to three times the size of honeybees and are black and yellow. They are not as social as honeybees, typically nesting in small colonies, usually underground, and are generally noted for being mild mannered and not easily disturbed. They seldom sting. Their stinger is barbless.

### Signs and Symptoms

Other than the signs and symptoms listed earlier in this chapter, a victim with a systemic reaction to a bee sting may experience vomiting, diarrhea, headache, fever, muscle spasms, breathing difficulty, maybe even convulsions.

### Treatment

Needless to say, it is important to remove a bee's stinger as soon as possible. Although for many years it was widely and devoutly believed (and still is by some) that squeezing the embedded bee stinger and attached venom sac would squirt more venom into the sting site, the method of removal does not matter in the least. Here, speed is your best option. Just get the stinger out, any way you can, as fast as you can. For all other considerations, see the treatment section earlier in this chapter.

### A Closer Look: Bee Stinger Removal

The *Lancet* volume 348, pages 301–2, states: "Weal size and thus envenomization increased as the time from stinging to removal of the sting increased, even within seconds. There was no difference in the response to stings which were scraped or pinched off after two seconds . . . immediate treatment of bee stings should emphasize quick removal without concern regarding the method of removal."

### Prevention

If confronted by a bee or two, stay calm and back away slowly. They do not appear to like rapid movements, especially swatting movements. If attacked by a swarm, run for dense cover, lie face down, and cover your head with your hands. Bright-colored summer clothing seems to attract winged insects, especially bees. Tan, light brown, white, and light green clothes appear to have no special appeal, but bees can be attracted by open containers of anything sweet. Insect repellents do *not* work.

## A Closer Look: "Killer" Bees

The famed "killer" bees, near relatives of honeybees and virtually impossible to tell apart, were introduced to Brazil from Africa around the 1950s because they were thought to be better honey makers in tropical regions. Being committed to swarming often and great at traveling long distances, they entered the extreme southern United States in October 1990. Killer bee venom is no more potent than honeybee venom, and they actually inject slightly less venom per sting than honeybees. But killers are noted for mass attacks by hundreds of individual bees with little provocation—and they will continue the attack over a great distance once they get agitated. Some experts estimate that approximately sixty human deaths per year are currently being caused by killer bees.

## WASPS

In many regions, wasp family members, including hornets and yellow jackets, are more likely to sting than bees, at least partially because some species tend to build their nests on or near human dwellings. Only females have stingers. If they feel threatened or if they feel their nest is threatened, they are more aggressive, generally speaking, than bees. Wasp stingers are barbless, and one wasp can inflict multiple stings. Their venom is not only for defense but also for the killing of prey—but it takes somewhere around 100 stings to create a potentially fatal reaction in people. Human death by multiple wasp stings is very rare, but death by anaphylaxis from wasp venom is not rare. Unlike bees, wasps are predators and scavengers that are attracted to meat and decaying matter. Garbage, in other words, invites them to visit.

Yellow jackets grow to about 0.6 inch (1 centimeter or so) in length and have bright yellow and black stripes. They tend to be bold, persistent, and aggressive, more aggressive than other hymenopterans. A nest may house up to 3000 individuals, and many will swarm out to deliver multiple stings in a brief amount of time if the nest is disturbed.

*Figure 7.2 Yellow Jacket*

### Treatment
Wasps' dirty stingers have a higher rate of infection, and the site of their stings should be thoroughly cleaned.

### Prevention
Other than avoiding nests, wasp stings can be prevented by taking precautions similar to those that help prevent bee stings.

**Fascinating Facts**

The social wasps, such as paper wasps, bald-faced hornets, and yellow jackets, build their elaborate nests out of paper that they make. They chew up fragments of wood and leaves that mix with their saliva to create paper.

## FIRE ANTS

Ants are found worldwide, and many species are capable of delivering a painful sting. In the United States, only one species *(Solenopsis invicta)* carries medical significance in its venom. Not an indigenous insect, the notoriously aggressive fire ant has spread like kudzu since it first appeared in Alabama in the 1920s. Way down south, from North Carolina across to Texas, in the warm summer months, beware of a small reddish brown to black ant (see Figure 7.3) that lives in mounds. Unsuspecting humans who step on a mound can find their legs covered in hundreds of ants within 30 seconds. Unlike most ants, fire ants attack instead of running away.

*Figure 7.3 Fire Ant*

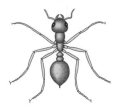

Sharp mandibles attach the ant to your skin, but the mild pain of the bite only marks the beginning of an enraged fire ant attack. While holding on, the ant jabs in its rear-end-positioned stinger, releases venom, pulls out the stinger, twists, and jabs again. It will keep jabbing until you swat it off. If you do not swat, it will sting a ring of extraordinarily painful, burning wounds.

Although most people get over fire ant stings by cursing and scratching, serious reactions are not uncommon. During the famous Fire Ant Summer of 1971, more than 6,000 victims were treated for infections from stings. On the more serious end of treatment that year, 76 people had severe allergic responses, 8 needed skin grafts, and 5 had body parts amputated. Deaths due to anaphylaxis may run as high as 30 humans per year.

### Signs and Symptoms
Pain from a fire ant attack usually keeps the victim's teeth clinched for about an hour. Over the next few hours, swelling develops and a clear, fluid-filled bump appears where each sting occurred. Bumps can itch for a week.

### Treatment
The application of cold may ease the pain for a short while. Some products claim to ease the symptoms—and you could find they work for you. But a few experts suggest that no medications have proven effective in either relieving the symptoms or preventing the fluid-filled bumps.

### Prevention
If you are attacked by a hoard of fire ants, running and swatting are both approved methods of fighting back. But the best way to avoid an attack is to watch where you walk.

CHAPTER 8.

# Miscellaneous Biters and Stingers

**IMAGINE THIS:**
*Your child walks into your campsite, holding in the palm of her hand a furry caterpillar curled up as if asleep. It is sort of appealing to watch the small child fascinated with the small fur ball. But suddenly she screams in pain, throwing the caterpillar from her. Her hand begins to swell and turn red. Can caterpillars bite? What should you do?*

## BEETLES

Beetles (order Coleoptera) make up the largest group of insects, with approximately 250,000 known species. All have mouthparts designed for chewing, and some can deliver a bite and some a sting—but there is no beetle venom, from bite or sting, that has proven dangerous to humans. Small beetles of several species have been known to crawl into human ears and inflict nasty damage chewing on the ear canal and eardrum.

Blister beetles (family Meloidae), however, relatively widespread in the United States, exude a toxin called cantharidin when disturbed or squeezed. This secretion penetrates human skin. There are numerous species of blister beetles. They are generally medium-sized, growing to about a half inch (15 millimeters), with soft forewings. Some are dark, and some are colored rather brilliantly.

**Fascinating Facts**

The juice of blister beetles, specifically the toxin cantharidin, has been thought to be an aphrodisiac by some people, who ingested it to improve their love life. Ingestion produces nausea, vomiting, diarrhea, and stomach cramps, none of which are reportedly sensuous.

### Signs and Symptoms

Contact with the toxin cantharidin does not produce pain, but 2 to 5 hours later, single or multiple blisters appear. These blisters are also painless unless they are rubbed and broken open. Illness has been rarely reported in some humans who were heavily blistered by these beetles.

### Treatment

Nothing specific seems to work to speed disappearance of the blisters. They seem to respond best when treated as small burns.

### Prevention

In terms of preventing the blisters, little is known other than keeping your eyes open and avoiding contact with the beetles.

## CATERPILLARS

Caterpillars (order Lepidoptera) are larval insects waiting to metamorphose into butterflies or moths. While waiting, some lepidopterans—about sixteen families worldwide—are venomous. Venomous caterpillars have nothing distinctive to help you identify them: Many are flat and sluggish, some are thickly covered in long hairs and some with spiny hairs, and some are bright in color while others hide using camouflage.

Caterpillars use their venom not to attack but only to defend themselves. The venom comes from spines that may be spread over the body of the bug, mixed with nonvenomous hairs, or grouped together. The nastiest of poisonous caterpillars has hollow spines with a venom gland at the base and a tiny muscle surrounding the gland that may assist in pushing out the poison. They sting, therefore, rather than bite.

In the United States, from Maryland across Missouri to Texas and points south, the most significantly poisonous caterpillar is the puss caterpillar, or woolly slug, looking something like a curled-up pussycat—and thus its name. Instant pain, often described as pulsing, follows the sting.

## *Figure 8.1 Puss Caterpillar*

**Important Note**

The venom of dead stinging caterpillars remains active. Even the offending spines, separate from the caterpillar, may cause a reaction.

Relatives of the puss caterpillar, including New England's flannel moth caterpillar, deliver less-severe but still-painful stings. Other stinging caterpillars of the United States include but are not limited to the gypsy moth caterpillar, the io moth caterpillar, the saddleback caterpillar, and the tussock caterpillar.

### Signs and Symptoms

Redness, swelling, and itching typically develop from a caterpillar sting. A rash is common. Symptoms may last up to 24 hours, and the pain can be intense. Nausea, vomiting, fever, headache, difficulty breathing, convulsions, and shock have been reported, but not often.

### Treatment

In the case of a caterpillar sting, remove the spines that are still stuck in the victim's skin as soon as possible. Any sticky tape will help in spine removal. Corticosteroid creams or ointments should ease local reactions. If more serious complications develop, see a doctor. Those victims with serious reactions usually end up being treated in a hospital and released without any permanent damage.

### Prevention

Avoidance is the only prevention.

### Caterpillars of Other Nations

Some caterpillars outside the United States, such as the members of the genus *Lonomia,* a resident of South American tropical forests, are well documented to have caused deaths in a few humans. Other caterpillars are known to cause rather intense pain with redness and swelling, and occasionally systemic reactions such as nausea, fever, and chills. Painkillers have been effective, but otherwise no specific treatments have proven of any special worth.

## CENTIPEDES AND MILLIPEDES

Centipedes have one pair of legs per body segment, and body segments number from at least 15 to more than 100—as their name implies. Some species reach a length of about 1 foot (30 centimeters). All centipedes have a pair of curved hollow fangs in their first segment that are attached to venom glands. Although centipedes use their venom primarily for acquiring food—they kill and consume invertebrates in most cases, but small vertebrates in some cases—they will bite humans if threatened. Any centipede with fangs capable of piercing human skin will cause a local reaction with its venom.

Millipedes are significantly different from centipedes (see Figure 8.2). For one thing, millipedes have two pairs of legs per body segment. And for another thing, none of the millipedes have a method for injecting venom. Although all millipedes in the United States are considered harmless, in some parts of the world, especially the tropics, millipedes can eject a potent defensive chemical that burns and may cause blisters.

### Signs and Symptoms

Be prepared, if a centipede does bite, for burning pain with increasing redness and swelling. Bites may be tender for up to two weeks.

*Figure 8.2 Centipede and Millipede*

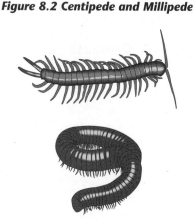

### Treatment

Because centipede bites are considered nonthreatening to life and limb, no particular treatment has ever been developed. Some people report that washing the wound with ammonia helps relieve the pain, and other painkilling drugs would be appropriate to use. Of greater importance is thoroughly cleaning the wound of a centipede bite, and tetanus prophylaxis should be up to date. Infection rates are high in uncleaned bites.

### Prevention

To prevent injuries from centipedes, one must watch where naked hands and feet are placed.

# Selected References

## CHAPTER 1. DANGEROUS REPTILES

Ernst, Carl H. *Venomous Reptiles of North America.* Washington, D.C.: Smithsonian Institution Press, 1999.

Forgey, William, MD. "Reptile Envenomizations." Chap. 20 in *Wilderness Medical Society Practice Guidelines for Wilderness Emergency Care.* Guilford, Conn.: The Globe Pequot Press, 2001.

Gold, Barry, MD, Richard Dart, MD, Ph.D., and Robert Barish, MD. "Bites of venomous reptiles." *The New England Journal of Medicine* 347, no. 5 (August 1, 2002): 347-356 www.nejm.org.

Norris, Robert Jr., MD, and Sean Bush, MD. "North American Venomous Reptile Bites." Chap. 38 in *Wilderness Medicine*, 4th ed., edited by Paul Auerbach, MD. St Louis, Mo.: Mosby, Inc., 2001.

Sutherland, Struan, MD, and Guy Nolch. "Snakes." In *Dangerous Australian Animals.* Flemington, Victoria, Australia: Hyland House Publishing, 2000.

Whitaker, Romulus. *Common Indian Snakes.* New Delhi, India: Macmillan India Ltd., 1978.

## CHAPTER 2. DANGEROUS SPIDERS

Stewart, Charles E., MD. "Bites and Stings." Chap. 7 in *Environmental Emergencies.* Baltimore, Md.: Williams and Wilkins, 1990.

Sutherland, Struan, MD, and Guy Nolch. "Spiders and Other Arachnids." In *Dangerous Australian Animals.* Flemington, Victoria, Australia: Hyland House Publishing, 2000.

## CHAPTER 3. DANGEROUS SCORPIONS

Suchard, Jeffery, MD, and David Connor, MD. "Scorpion Envenomization." Chap. 35 in *Wilderness Medicine*, 4th ed., edited by Paul Auerbach, MD. St Louis, Mo.: Mosby, Inc., 2001.

Wilkerson, James, MD. "Bites and Stings." Chap. 25 in *Medicine for Mountaineering & Other Wilderness Activities*, 5th ed. Seattle, Wash.: The Mountaineers Books, 2001.

## CHAPTER 4. TICKS

Gentile, Douglas, MD, and Jason Lang, MD. "Tick-Borne Diseases." Chap. 33 in *Wilderness Medicine*, 4th ed., edited by Paul Auerbach, MD. St Louis, Mo.: Mosby, Inc., 2001.

## CHAPTER 5. MOSQUITOES

Fradin, Mark, MD, and John Day, Ph.D. "Comparative efficacy of insect repellents against mosquito bites." *The New England Journal of Medicine* 347 no. 1 (July 4, 2002):13–18. www.nejm.org.

Rose, Stuart, MD. "Insect-Bite Protection." Chap. 7 in *International Travel Health Guide*, 12th ed. Northampton, Mass.: Travel Medicine, Inc., 2001.

———. "Insect-Borne Diseases." Chap. 8 in *International Travel Health Guide*, 12th ed. Northampton, Mass.: Travel Medicine, Inc., 2001.

## CHAPTER 6. MORE BLOOD-FEEDING ARTHROPODS

Howarth, Jane Wilson, MD. "Getting Bitten to Death." In *Bugs, Bites and Bowels*. Guilford, Conn.: The Globe Pequot Press, 1995.

———. "Dangerous and Unpleasant Animals." In *Bugs, Bites and Bowels*. Guilford, Conn.: The Globe Pequot Press, 1995.

Jong, Elaine, MD, and Russell McMullen, MD. *The Travel and Tropical Medicine Manual*. Philadelphia, Pa.: W. B. Saunders Co., 1995.

Stewart, Charles E., MD. "Bites and Stings." Chap. 7 in *Environmental Emergencies*. Baltimore, Md.: Williams and Wilkins, 1990.

## CHAPTER 7. THE STINGING ARTHROPODS

Minton, Sherman, MD, Bernard Bechtel, MD, and Timothy Erickson, MD. "North American Arthropod Envenomization and Parasitism." Chap. 36 in *Wilderness Medicine*, 4th ed., edited by Paul Auerbach, MD. St Louis, Mo.: Mosby, Inc., 2001.

## CHAPTER 8. MISCELLANEOUS BITERS AND STINGERS

Forgey, William, MD. "Arthropod Envenomizations." Chap. 21 in *Wilderness Medical Society Practice Guidelines for Wilderness Emergency Care*. Guilford, Conn.: The Globe Pequot Press, 2001.

THE MOUNTAINEERS, founded in 1906, is a nonprofit outdoor activity and conservation club, whose mission is "to explore, study, preserve, and enjoy the natural beauty of the outdoors. . . . " Based in Seattle, Washington, the club is now the third-largest such organization in the United States, with 15,000 members and five branches throughout Washington State.

The Mountaineers sponsors both classes and year-round outdoor activities in the Pacific Northwest, which include hiking, mountain climbing, ski-touring, snowshoeing, bicycling, camping, kayaking and canoeing, nature study, sailing, and adventure travel. The club's conservation division supports environmental causes through educational activities, sponsoring legislation, and presenting informational programs. All club activities are led by skilled, experienced volunteers, who are dedicated to promoting safe and responsible enjoyment and preservation of the outdoors.

If you would like to participate in these organized outdoor activities or the club's programs, consider a membership in The Mountaineers. For information and an application, write or call The Mountaineers, Club Headquarters, 300 Third Avenue West, Seattle, WA 98119; 206-284-6310.

The Mountaineers Books, an active, nonprofit publishing program of the club, produces guidebooks, instructional texts, historical works, natural history guides, and works on environmental conservation. All books produced by The Mountaineers Books fulfill the club's mission.

***Send or call for our catalog of more than 500 outdoor titles:***

The Mountaineers Books
1001 SW Klickitat Way, Suite 201
Seattle, WA 98134
800-553-4453
*mbooks@mountaineersbooks.org*
*www.mountaineersbooks.org*

The Mountaineers Books is proud to be a corporate sponsor of Leave No Trace, whose mission is to promote and inspire responsible outdoor recreation through education, research, and partnerships. The Leave No Trace program is focused specifically on human-powered (nonmotorized) recreation.

Leave No Trace strives to educate visitors about the nature of their recreational impacts, as well as offer techniques to prevent and minimize such impacts. Leave No Trace is best understood as an educational and ethical program, not as a set of rules and regulations.

For more information, visit *www.LNT.org,* or call 800-332-4100.

## OTHER TITLES YOU MIGHT ENJOY FROM THE MOUNTAINEERS BOOKS

Available at fine bookstores and outdoor stores, by phone at 800-553-4453, or on the Web at *www.mountaineersbooks.org*

*Don't Get Eaten: The Dangers of Animals that Charge or Attack* by Dave Smith. $6.95 paperbound. 0-89886-912-9.

*Don't Get Sick: The Hidden Dangers of Camping and Hiking* by Buck Tilton, M.S. and Rick Bennett, Ph.D. $8.95 paperbound. 0-89886-854-8.

*First Aid: A Pocket Guide, 4th Edition* by Christopher Van Tilburg, M.D. $3.50 paperbound. 0-89886-719-3.

*Emergency Survival: A Pocket Guide* by Christopher Van Tilburg, M.D. $3.50 paperbound. 0-89886-768-1.

*Staying Found: The Complete Map & Compass Handbook, 3rd Edition* by June Fleming. $12.95 paperbound. 0-89886-785-1.

*Wilderness Navigation: Finding Your Way Using Map, Compass, Altimeter, & GPS* by Mike Burns and Bob Burns. $9.95 paperbound. 0-89886-629-4.

*GPS Made Easy: Using Global Positioning Systems in the Outdoors, 3rd Edition* by Lawrence Letham. $14.95 paperbound. 0-89886-802-5.

*Backcountry Bear Basics: The Definitive Guide to Avoiding Unpleasant Encounters* by David Smith. $10.95 paperbound. 0-89886-500-X.

*Kids in the Wild: A Family Guide to Outdoor Recreation* by Cindy Ross and Todd Gladfelter. $12.95 paperbound. 0-89886-447-X.

*Everyday Wisdom: 1001 Expert Tips for Hikers* by Karen Berger. $16.95 paperbound. 0-89886-523-9.

*Outdoor Leadership: Technique, Common Sense & Self-Confidence* by John Graham. $16.95 paperbound. 0-89886-502-6.

*Conditioning for Outdoor Fitness: A Comprehensive Training Guide* by David Musnick, M.D. and Mark Pierce, A.T.C. $21.95 paperbound. 0-89886-450-X.

*Photography Outdoors: A Field Guide for Travel & Adventure Photographers, 2nd Edition* by Mark Gardner and Art Wolfe. $14.95 paperbound. 0-89886-888-2.